THE SERVICE TRAP
FROM ALTRUISM TO DIRTY WORK

PAULA DRESSEL, Ph.D.

Department of Sociology
Georgia State University
Atlanta, Georgia

More than a how-to manual for social workers, this book describes and highlights many of the frustrations faced by service providers, provides insights into everyday problems, and suggests changes in the field. Students, educators, practitioners, and researchers in all service professions will appreciate the insights provided into the effects of impersonal policy decisions and administrative regulations. The implementation of social welfare policies, cultural and historical bases of current welfare initiatives, future prospects for service workers in light of reduced welfare commitments, and the use of role manipulation, role bargaining, norm violations, quasi theories, and comparisons by social workers in coping with work-related problems are among the specific topics discussed.

CHARLES C THOMAS • PUBLISHER • SPRINGFIELD • ILLINOIS

THE SERVICE TRAP

THE SERVICE TRAP

FROM ALTRUISM TO DIRTY WORK

By

PAULA DRESSEL, Ph.D.

Department of Sociology
Georgia State University
Atlanta, Georgia

CHARLES C THOMAS • PUBLISHER
Springfield • Illinois • U.S.A.

Published and Distributed Throughout the World by

CHARLES C THOMAS • PUBLISHER
2600 South First Street
Springfield, Illinois 62717

© *1984 by* CHARLES C THOMAS • PUBLISHER

ISBN 0-398-04975-0

Library of Congress Catalog Card Number: 83-24089

Printed in the United States of America

SC-R-3

Library of Congress Cataloging in Publication Data

Dressel, Paula.
   The service trap.

   Bibliography: p.
   Includes index.
   1. Social service—United States.   I. Title.
HV95.D74   1984   361.3'0973   83-24089
ISBN 0-398-04975-0

To my family

PREFACE

This book represents the convergence of multiple issues that
have captured my attention over the last several years. During that time I have been fascinated by how social welfare legislation emerges from a morass of diverse specialized interests, from
public opinion characterized by ambivalence or contradiction,
and from the vested political interests of the decision makers
themselves. At the same time, my attention has been drawn to the
plight of welfare recipients of all types of backgrounds whose
collective circumstances do not alter appreciably, despite the historical trend of increasing allocations to the human services. In
addition, my professional contacts with service providers and administrators who implement welfare policies have enabled me to
appreciate the complexities and the difficulties of the work that
they carry out. When I looked more closely at the everyday world
of service work, the several interests just mentioned began to
converge in a meaningful and systematic way. It was then that I
came to understand the trap in which service workers find themselves as they go about their efforts to help others, and to see how
their responses to their situational dilemmas reproduce the very
welfare system that generates their difficulties.

The analysis presented in the following pages will be misunderstood if the reader concludes that service workers are to blame for
many of our welfare problems. Such an observation is tantamount
to blaming the victim. Rather, my intention is to demonstrate how
the constraints under which these women and men work lead to
short-term adaptive behaviors that are self-defeating over the long
term. The same argument can be made about individuals in other
areas of the welfare enterprise, politicians and organizational bureaucrats alike. The collective behaviors of all of these individuals
add up to a welfare system that is riddled with internally generated

vii

problems and that inadequately addresses the difficulties of targeted welfare beneficiaries.

I have deep respect for many service workers, administrators, and legislators who labor against all odds in their commitment to help others. Their dedication reflects "the persistence of the human drive for a more decent world" (Galper, 1975:77). I hope this book will help them understand why their going is so tough and will renew their hope that alternative paths are available in pursuit of that decent world.

THE AUDIENCE

This book is written with multiple constituencies in mind. While there is some concern about addressing a book to more than a single target audience, I have chosen to do so for two major reasons. First, it is my belief that students, professors, researchers, and practitioners will all have a professional interest in the issues raised in the following chapters. Insofar as they do, these issues will establish common ground for them to learn from one another's unique perspectives. Second, I believe there is enough commonality among the languages of these groups to be able to address them simultaneously. I would rather work on the basis of these assumptions than perpetuate arbitrary and artificial divisions among these groups.

Nevertheless, I expect that each group will approach the book with its own intentions, will emphasize different arguments or themes of the book, and will respond somewhat differently to them. Thus, I would like to provide my own suggestions for ways in which the book might be utilized more fruitfully by various audiences.

First, the book is intended for students and professors of social work, social welfare, political science, public administration, and social gerontology. For those in social work and social welfare, it offers an understanding of direct linkages between the day-to-day enterprise of doing social work and the larger dynamics of promoting social welfare. Attention is given both to how public policy influences the ability of service providers to carry out their work and how, in turn, the sum of providers' efforts reinforces or challenges the system of social welfare. While the book is not a how-to manual for would-be social workers or their instructors, its descriptions and analyses highlight many of the frustrations service providers are likely to encounter, offer insights into the sources of everyday problems, and provide suggestions for change in the occupation. And while the book is also not a policy compendium for social welfare specialists, it should be most useful to them in its discussions of the implementation of social welfare policies, the cultural and historical bases of current social welfare initiatives, and future prospects for service workers in light of reduced welfare commitments.

For students and professors of political science and public administration, this book offers insights into the day-to-day effects of seemingly impersonal policy decisions and their attendant administrative regulations. Such effects occur within various channels of implementation and between differently positioned human beings whose needs and satisfactions are not necessarily consistent with original policy intentions or with efficient, effective, or proper operationalization of particular policies. While no direct advice is provided to political analysts for guaranteeing either improved implementation processes or improved policies that respond to the human exigencies of implementation, they should be interested in the discussion of trade-offs for different constituencies in the social welfare enterprise if specific social reform efforts are undertaken.

Social gerontologists, who may also identify with one of the aforementioned disciplines, will have particular interest in the original data provided in the book, since these are interviews with direct service workers in the field of aging. Such readers are likely to be as interested in the specifics of the issues as in their general application. This specialized appeal, however, should not obscure the contention that the issues explored and the arguments raised throughout the book are generalizable to virtually all public social welfare undertakings. This is so because such undertakings occur within common organizational, cultural, and political frameworks at the same point in historical time.

This book is also intended for researchers in social welfare, sociology, and political science. All three groups may be interested in the attempt to draw together the micro and macro worlds of social service. Regarding the substance of the chapters, social welfare specialists are likely to be drawn to the interplay of the various arenas involved in carrying out the welfare enterprise: the general public, politicians, administrators, and direct service providers. Sociologists should find interesting the ways in which role manipulation, role bargaining, norm violations, quasi theories, and comparisons are utilized by service workers to cope with their work-related problems and frustrations. Of interest as well should be the ways in which these mechanisms collectively contribute to the reproduction of the status quo in social welfare policy and the reinforcement of public opinion and stereotypes regarding the recipients of welfare benefits and services. Political scientists may focus most readily on implementation issues; they may also be interested in the explication of a set of policy options and their various implications.

Finally, this book is addressed to those individuals, both line staff and supervisors, who are employed at the local level in public welfare services. In a real sense, this is their story. Many of these workers will readily identify with the situations described and the complaints rendered. Beyond that, it is hoped that these individuals will take away a new perspective on the sources of the problems they encounter in their day-to-day work lives. Further, some of the recommendations offered in the closing chapter may provide the impetus for social action on the part of these readers. The material offered in this book could be utilized in in-service training programs for systematic discussion of routinely encountered problems and for fundamental consciousness raising of service providers and their employers. While the focus of the book is on publicly funded services, there may be fruitful reading within these pages for privately funded service organization personnel as well. Specifically, it would be worthwhile reading for those private organizations considering application for public monies. Further, insofar as private organizations operate within the same cultural climate as do public services, some of the larger concerns pursued in the following pages will be applicable to them as well.

ACKNOWLEDGMENTS

The author wishes to thank the following individuals and organizations for their assistance with the various phases of the research project that underlies the book. Funding for the empirical research was provided through an Urban Life Grant from Georgia State University. Interviews were conducted by Callie Flanigan, Dottie Webber, and Jane Wood. Library research was performed by Tony Baker and Callie Flanigan. Typing assistance was provided by Patricia Hitt, Sherry Hood, and Joyce Johnson. While the service providers who were interviewed in the course of the research cannot be mentioned by name, of course, their contributions are gratefully acknowledged.

In addition, several individuals and offices should be recognized for their assistance in the development of this book. The Dean's Office in the College of Arts and Sciences at Georgia State University provided funds for the technical production of the manuscript. The monumental task of typing the many versions of the book was done by Joyce Johnson with back-up assistance from Jacquelyn Rosemond, both of the Department of Sociology at Georgia State. Library assistance was provided by David Whittier. The support of several colleagues should also be recognized: Gordon Walker, for his continuous encouragement; Gerald Suttles, for his critical feedback; Michael Lipsky, for his helpful conversations; and Robert Binstock, for his insistence on clarity. The shortcomings of the book, of course, are my responsibility alone.

Parts of chapters 2 and 5 are based on my article "Policy Sources of Worker Dissatisfactions: The Case of Human Services in Aging," (*Social Service Review* 56, 3[September, 1982]:406–423). Permission from The University of Chicago Press for utilization of that material is gratefully acknowledged.*

Social Service Review (September, 1952). ©1982 by The University of Chicago. All rights reserved.

CONTENTS

THE SERVICE TRAP

Chapter 1

THE TRAP OF SERVICE WORK
Setting the Stage

Despite dramatic growth in expenditures for social interventions in the past two decades, many social welfare problems remain entrenched. At the same time, new and pressing social concerns have emerged to compete for the nation's resources. As a consequence, social welfare as a public enterprise is being attacked from all sides by its many constituent groups: from politicians both liberal and conservative, from service providers* and administrators as well as service recipients, and from the general public in the forms of taxpayer revolts and ideological backlash.

While these groups may not agree about what is wrong with welfare or what should be done about it, they do agree on one thing: the welfare system is not faring well. The blame for social welfare failures comes from varied directions; multiple maladies have been diagnosed, and as many accompanying proposals for change have been proffered.

For example, conservative politicians argue for the retrenchment of public sector programs in favor of reliance on the private sector to alleviate human needs. Accordingly, they propose indirect measures for addressing social welfare issues through the stimulation of economic growth and the trickle-down benefits it is claimed to have for the needy. Further, these politicians concentrate on the need for efficiency and the elimination of waste and

---

*The terms "social service worker," "service worker," "social worker," and "service provider" are used interchangeably throughout the book. These designations may or may not refer to individuals with professional training in social work. Rather, they denote individuals who provide public services to targeted groups through direct contact with the target population. Of course, the use of this broad definition does not deny certain differences that may exist between professionally trained and paraprofessional human service workers (e.g., Freudenberger, 1976).

abuse in remaining social programs. In short, their focus for the failure of social interventions is an overly activist state that has propagated programs in scale and scope well beyond its appropriate domain.

On the other hand, liberal politicians cite the need for greater government involvement to remedy social welfare ills. Their viewpoint is that publicly sponsored social welfare programs can succeed, if only benefits are made more extensive, planning strategies more rational, and program funds more abundant. Further, they believe that various regulatory mechanisms must be instituted to correct for or to contain certain market dynamics that are dysfunctional for social welfare operations. In short, the source of liberals' blame for welfare inadequacies is reluctant government activism. Not surprisingly, those service providers and administrators employed in public programs are likely to side with liberal politicians in their assessment of what is wrong with welfare. They are confronted every day with needy clients, shortages of funds, and organizational dilemmas.

Welfare recipients are also dissatisfied. On a day-to-day basis, the likely sources of recipients' discontents with welfare are service providers who deny them benefits, question their integrity, and undermine their dignity. More diffusely, beneficiaries find fault with the welfare "system." The "system," in effect, represents the symbolic manifestation of troubling dynamics beyond recipients' face-to-face experiences. These dynamics include the passing of legislation that stigmatizes welfare clientele, the creating of arbitrary welfare regulations and guidelines, and the scapegoating of recipients for the internal problems of welfare organizations and the inherent shortcomings of welfare legislation.

The general public is ambivalent about public social welfare activities. On the one hand, because of their interest in social stability, if not social justice, they want reassurance that welfare problems are being addressed. On the other hand, citizens of diverse political persuasions realize that their tax dollars are not producing an adequate return on welfare investments, and they sense that the welfare system needs some kind of dramatic reform. Specific dimensions of their dissatisfactions with public welfare mimic issues articulated by both conservative and liberal politicians.

These diverse concerns from all sides are not unfounded. A nation that spends $350 to $400 billion annually on social programs ought to expect noticeable returns from its tax dollars. Instead of seeing the alleviation of public ills, however, the public is confronted with ongoing claims by groups whose plights remain virtually unaffected, by others whose conditions have actually worsened, and by yet others whose difficulties are newly emergent. In a perverse way, the successes of social welfare agencies have come to be measured by the sizes of the budgets they command rather than by the impact of their performance on public problems (Drucker, 1973).

What is wrong with the welfare system? Various authorities have focused on different areas within the welfare enterprise — public opinion, political decision making, organizational activity, and direct service delivery — in attempts to answer this question. For example, Howe (1978) and Cook (1979) examine the issue of public support for welfare activities. Both note citizens' distinctions between deserving and undeserving individuals and their unwillingness to endorse assistance for the latter. Other authors, e.g., Ogren (1973) and Smith and Spinrad (1981), call attention to the general ambivalence of the public toward governmental welfare functions. Binstock and Levin (1976) outline the political dilemmas surrounding the creation and implementation of policies for social intervention. They note that policy effectiveness is limited by the dynamics involved in getting welfare policies adopted as well as the difficulties encountered in their subsequent implementation. Pressman and Wildavsky (1973) detail the vagaries of program implementation, with its many unforeseen and deleterious consequences. In addition, Lipsky (1980) focuses attention on the dilemmas experienced by service providers in the everyday provision of welfare assistance. He argues that service workers' resolutions of everyday dilemmas represent policy making at the local level. Such resolutions, and the effects they have on service recipients, are not always supportive of the intentions of the original social policies.

In short, these studies analyze what goes wrong in various areas of the social welfare enterprise. To be sure, these analyses have been helpful for understanding the problems, dilemmas, and constraints operating in those areas. What has been lacking, however, is an understanding of how the interactions of these areas with one another generate even more problems for the operation of the welfare system. The inability to resolve these problems exacerbates social welfare failures.

The task of this book is to illuminate some of the connections among the areas of the welfare system. Theoretically, analysis could begin at any of the areas or subsystems. However, the primary vantage point for understanding the connections among subsystems is the everyday world of direct service providers. The practical reason for this perspective derives from having had direct access to this area through intensive interviews with service personnel. However, there are conceptual justifications for such a vantage point that are far more important.

First, any macrophenomenon, in this case the welfare system, is comprised at heart of "aggregations and repetitions of many similar microevents" (Collins, 1981:988). The welfare "system" is an abstraction summarizing a complex array of individual and group behaviors. Focusing on the everyday world of service providers allows an intimate examination of one set of microbehaviors on which the welfare system is recreated day in and day out. Further, if the welfare system is to change, "it is because the(se) individuals . . . change their microbehaviors" (Collins, 1981:989).

The second conceptual justification for the focal point lies in the fact that individuals who deliver services to welfare recipients are located at the intersection of the potentially conflicting subsystems of the welfare enterprise. Service providers must manage the various demands made by official decision makers, whose policies they implement; by agency administrators, whose employees they are; by service recipients, whose caretakers, defenders, and advocates they are expected to be; and by the general public, whose values about social welfare in part shape and are shaped by what occurs at the level of direct services. In addition, service providers bring their own personal expectations to the work situation. The vantage point of the service delivery agent first allows a look at the area in which the competing imperatives of these groups are played out. In addition, starting from this point gives access, either directly or indirectly, to all of the other subsystems that comprise the service enterprise.

Finally, there is conceptual justification for the vantage point from the argument that service providers, in effect, make social welfare policy (Lipsky, 1978, 1980). How they manage the various demands made upon them ultimately determines how social welfare initiatives are translated to clientele and the general public. In short, service workers are central agents in the social welfare enterprise.

The connections that are made in the following chapters between the area of service delivery and the other subsystems of the welfare enterprise lead to the conclusion that service workers are caught in a trap created from the cross-pressures of these subsystems. In trying to resolve the conflicting demands from these areas, service providers behave in ways that inadvertently tighten the trap. That is, the specific strategies they employ for coping with conflicting demands serve instead to enhance their difficulties, perpetuate welfare inadequacies, and lend credibility to critics of the welfare system. This is a fundamental irony of social service work.

This book is based on three central arguments. The first argument is that the work of human service providers in public agencies is riddled with ongoing tensions, conflicts, and frustrations that are highly predictable. The same kinds of work-related complaints are expressed by service workers regardless of where they work, what services they provide, and whose needs they address. This suggests that workers' problems do not stem from their personal work styles or their employer's managerial approach, as some writers argue. Rather, because the same kinds of problems arise across agencies and throughout different services, the sources of service worker difficulties must be sought in systems beyond individual personalities and managerial styles.

Therefore, the second argument is that many of the problems service providers encounter originate in other areas of the welfare system. Specifically, these problems emerge because of the ways that organizational, political, and cultural imperatives get played out in everyday service provision. In short, service worker problems should be seen as public issues:

Issues have to do with matters that transcend the local environments of the individual and the range of his inner life. They have to do with the organization of many such milieu into the institutions of an historical society as a whole, with the ways in which various milieu overlap and interpenetrate to form the larger structure of social and historical life. (Mills, 1959:8)

Workers' interactions with the subsystems of the larger social welfare structure provide the substance of the second argument.

The third argument of this book is that service workers' ways of coping with the problems they encounter in their day-to-day routines are self-defeating. Service providers more often than not develop personalized coping strategies that in the short-term alleviate personal stress; however, in the longer run these coping mechanisms serve to reinforce the very welfare system from which the problems initially emerged. Sieber (1981) refers to this sort of self-defeating behavior as a fatal remedy. Not only is the remedy fatal for service workers, who get caught in a trap, such behavior also deflects attention from fundamental problems of the social welfare system that structure it for failure.

In sum, the following chapters present service providers as an important link in the welfare system. To be sure, many of the problems of their everyday work originate in decisions or indecisions made in other areas of the welfare enterprise. However, far from being impotent actors, they contribute significantly to the workings of the larger system by the way they respond to the dilemmas and contradictions they encounter.

An examination of the problems of service providers within the context of service organizations, policy structures, and the larger culture offers a broad-based picture of what is wrong with social welfare. As such, it provides at least tentative answers to the following issues:

- How do service workers, who are employed to alleviate social problems, instead contribute to the problems of the welfare system?
- Why do welfare organizations, regardless of the expertise of their personnel, encounter problems in the implementation of human services?
- How do our social welfare policies, designed to address

the difficulties of various populations, create problems and dilemmas for the population of service providers and administrators?

• What are the inherent constraints on welfare success in the United States?

• What measures can realistically bring improvement to the social welfare enterprise and to the task of service delivery?

The following chapters are organized according to the various areas of the welfare system. Chapter 2 looks at the everyday world of service work through the personal accounts of service providers themselves. Through their own statements, the inherent contradictions and conflicts of their work can be seen. Chapter 3 examines the organizational areas in which service work is carried out to see how organizational imperatives contribute to workers' difficulties. This chapter explores the implications of workers caught in the middle between the clients they are employed to serve and the agency administrators who employ them. Next, Chapter 4 discusses how politics, guided by public opinion and historical momentum, as well as its own internal imperatives, generates conflicts and contradictions for service personnel. Focus then returns to the everyday world of the service worker. Chapter 5 looks at the strategies used by service providers to manage the various tensions produced by other welfare subsystems; it explores the behavioral and symbolic ways in which they get by in their work and the consequences of their coping patterns for the larger social welfare enterprise. Attention is directed in the final chapter to current and future prospects for social welfare and for service workers. Implications of reduced public commitments to welfare functions are explored; the trade-offs of alternative initiatives are assessed. In essence, possible ways out of the service trap that would enhance the performance of social welfare functions in the United States are discussed.

The methodology for this book is both empirically and conceptually based. The core data that provide the direct quotations in Chapters 2 and 5 come from the author's intensive semistructured interviews with service providers in the field of aging. (Appendix A details the research design of that study; Appendix B provides the interview guidelines.) These data are corroborated with citations from research in other service areas such as child care, AFDC, police services, mental health counseling, and public school teaching. The analytic categories used in Chapters 2 and 5 derive from the qualitative research strategy of arranging and rearranging bits of interview data until conceptual patterns emerge (Lofland, 1971).

Chapters 3 and 4 represent an attempt to understand what was learned in the interviews from a systems perspective. The point is to link the everyday world of service work to other welfare subsystems. The analysis in these two chapters draws on literature in social policy, social welfare, social work, social organization, and social gerontology.

The final chapter utilizes implementation estimates (Hargrove, 1975) to analyze the likely success or failure of recently adopted as well as proposed social welfare legislation. Implementation estimates are the reasonable and likely difficulties and outcomes of putting social policies into effect. A second emphasis of Chapter 6 is the discussion of policy alternatives for alleviating the stressful conditions of service workers and, by implication, for improving the performance of the social welfare system. This part is based on a creative application of the literature in several substantive areas to a systems understanding of service work.

In sum, the arguments in this book are based both on original and secondary empirical data about the everyday tasks of helping people and on the creative linkage of those data to the literature on organizational dynamics, political decision making, and the foundations of public opinion.

THE SITUATIONAL CONTEXT

Before proceeding to the arguments, it is useful to provide the situational context for the discussion that follows. The day-to-day experiences of social welfare work will be described briefly. This description is generic; that is, it is meant to characterize the typical tasks of service provision. While cognizant of the variations that may occur across individuals, organizations, and service networks, it is not necessary to include them here. The intention is to suggest the flavor of the everyday roles and responsibilities of service workers and to set the behavioral context in which the points of the subsequent chapters are played out.

The typical tasks of human service providers in public agencies are organized around three temporal frameworks: daily routines, monthly events, and annual cycles. While all monthly events and annual cycles, of course, get played out as an accumulation of daily routines, the former temporal boundaries contain responsibilities in addition to those typical of daily experiences.

Daily routines consist of work-related experiences encountered by service providers during their everyday wakened state. Notice that daily service routines are not framed by clock-bound hours or by events occurring only at one's main employment location. This is purposeful, since many service workers utilize what otherwise might be their private time away from work (Zerubavel, 1979a) to perform work-related activities.

Much of service providers' daily routine consists of two inter-related types of work: casework, or service provision in direct contact with clients, and its accompanying paperwork. In many instances service personnel perform casework responsibilities away from the agency office. Therefore, traveling is an integral part of one's workday, even after having arrived at the central workplace. Paperwork tasks are typically undertaken at the office or at a service site. Frequently some portion of one's workday is spent at meetings: agency staff meetings, training workshops, or case coordination conferences. At the end of the formal workday, a service provider at home may still accept telephone calls from clients, try to catch up on caseload paperwork, or make preparations for the occupational demands of the following day.

Portions of daily routine are scheduled and predictable. Appointments are made with clients and colleagues, paperwork deadlines are established, and meetings are arranged with some advance notice. However, the nature of service work dictates that certain unanticipated situations will arise in the course of daily routine. Clients may experience emergencies; quickly arranged staff meetings may be called to handle unforeseen contingencies; plans may have to be changed on an ad hoc basis if fellow service providers cannot deliver the assistance upon which one's own service work is predicated. In sum, while each day of service work has a discernible pattern of events associated with it, daily routine is not inexorably fixed, and daily responsibilities may have to be reprioritized and rescheduled instantaneously.

Monthly events occur in addition to and simultaneously with day-to-day responsibilities. Service workers are expected to prepare summary information for monthly reports at the same time that they pursue their standing daily obligations. During months with recognized holidays, special service activities are likely to be undertaken. Events such as Thanksgiving, Christmas, Senior Citizens month, and the like will increase demands on service personnel that must be synchronized with the ongoing demands of daily routine.

Annual cycles add a further layer of activities to those already mentioned. Most notable in this regard are the responsibilities associated with yearly funding cycles. Responsibilities include preparation of a detailed annual report of one's activities for use in developing budget recommendations and establishing agency accountability to funders. Further, annual budget concerns may dictate that service workers attend public hearings and mobilize their clients to do the same to make the agency's case for additional funding.

Public agencies typically are financed through several different funding sources. The annual cycles of these sources do not always coincide. For instance, an agency may receive funds from the state whose fiscal year begins in July, from the federal government whose fiscal year starts in October, and from private sources who allocate monies every January. As a result, this agency will be required to operate within three separate annual cycles. Thus, additional service worker responsibilities that are tied to annual cycles may recur more than once each year. Service providers' tasks become more complex as the number of annual cycles in which their agency is embedded increases.

In sum, the work of service providers is organized across three simultaneously occurring temporal frameworks: daily routines, monthly events, and annual cycles. Predictable activities occur within each of these boundaries. In addition, the nature of service work generates unpredictable demands from both clients and the employing agency. Unexpected tasks must be articulated with planned activities in order to fulfill the complement of expectations associated with being a social worker.

With this context in mind, attention may be directed to the main thesis of this book: that service work is a trap for its dedicated servants and foremost agents. Workers' responses to the dilemmas of their work play a central role in the maintenance of the nation's inadequate welfare initiatives.

Chapter 2

THE EVERYDAY WORLD OF SERVICE WORK
Contradictions and Conflicts

A merican society has a rich history of people helping one
another. From the early forms of church aid and private
charities to present-day governmental dominance of welfare functions, the United States has long been characterized by formal
efforts to ameliorate distressful situations of individuals, families,
and groups. The experience of helping people has grown over
time from a purely volunteer effort into a professional and increasingly public endeavor.

While the literature about social welfare continues to grow, one
writer claims that "[w]e know much more about the experiences
and problems of the clients than we do about the experiences and
problems of the helpers" (Cherniss, 1978:2). Elsewhere he (Cherniss,
1980b:188) states: "For too long, we have been exclusively concerned with the emotional well-being of the client and have ig-
nored the needs, motivation, and morale of those who provide the
service." More critically, Rainwater (1967:2) maintains that

> Americans are, in general, indifferent to the welfare of their public
> functionaries—witness the notoriously poor prestige and salaries of
> these functionaries. . . . [S]ilence and ignorance [exist] about exactly what
> these functionaries are expected to do and how in fact they carry out
> society's . . . orders. . . .

There are at least two important reasons for taking a closer look
at service providers. First, as detailed later, and as others have
argued in different contexts (e.g., Zimmerman, 1969; Maslach,
1976; Cherniss, 1978; Larson et al., 1978; Maslach and Jackson,
1979; Maslach, 1979; Rooney, 1980), an understanding of service
workers' daily experiences, especially their work-related stresses,
provides insights into the quality of the human service experience.

14

Second, an intimate examination of the everyday world of service work illuminates how the seemingly impersonal welfare system gets played out on a day-to-day, face-to-face basis and how the collective actions of thousands of welfare providers accumulate into the societal function called social welfare.

One way of summarizing the professional literature on service providers and their work is to discuss three salient issues. First, certain studies address the images and functions of service workers; second, others contrast the provision of services in public versus private organizational settings; most recently a host of studies about service worker stresses has emerged under the popular label of *professional burnout*. These issues will be examined briefly.

With regard to service worker images and functions, two models have been widely articulated. These are representations of the service worker as altruist and, alternatively, as dirty worker (Rainwater, 1967).

The altruist model reflects an image that many have come to associate with professional social workers. According to this model, service providers are "responsive to a 'dedicatory ethic' " (Pines and Kafry, 1978:499); they are "essentially humanitarians" (Billingsley et al., 1966:53); they are "sympathetic, understanding, unselfish and helpful to others" (Registt, 1970:11); and the work they do represents a "calling" (Cherniss, 1980b:50; Gustafson, 1982; Kadushin, 1974:706). In addition, service work is believed to be characterized by autonomy, interesting and varied work responsibilities, and grateful clientele. While income potential for human service workers is relatively low, these job characteristics are seen as compensation for the poor wage scale (Cherniss et al., in press). However, some believe that the altruist model is more fiction than fact and refer to such a characterization of service work as a "professional mystique." They argue that belief in its existence in social work practice has dysfunctions for service providers (Cherniss et al., in press), who are not prepared for the disappointments and frustrations of the actual work.

The dirty worker model (Rainwater, 1967), on the other hand, maintains that, instead of actually helping people, service providers unwittingly operate to perpetuate a welfare system that creates client problems (*see* Galper, 1975). Under this model the service worker is not seen as a cruel individual who has "deliberately decided to harm or destroy families or children," operating from an agency reflecting a "conspiracy of a small group" (Wasserman, 1971:93). On the contrary, the service worker is a "mindless functionary" whose work reflects the banality of evil (Arendt, 1964), and is merely a vehicle for expressing the "profound hypocrisy of a larger society" (Wasserman, 1971:93). Service workers buffer the rest of society from potentially disruptive welfare recipients. In turn, clients come to view service providers as the source of their own frustrations with the welfare system; however, service workers themselves may be victims of that same system. Levy (1970:175) describes this double victimization in the following manner:

> What can be seen as the application of a social policy towards the poor stemming from the class and caste structure of American society and the organization of its institutions, become for the client an individualized and personalized event. The investigator is then viewed as "mean" or "nice" in the eyes of the client, as society, in the process of its political pie-splitting sets the general tone of the experience. Welfare workers . . . are bought off by society and conned into performing a crucial task which few wish to perform, that is doling out pennies to the poor on society's terms and "cooling them off" when they want more.

The two typologies of service work have their counterparts in descriptions of service organizations. The human service organization that is the vehicle for altruism is characterized by client centeredness, the systemic integration of services, the availability of comprehensive service offerings, and ready and equal accessibility for all potential clientele (Baker, 1974). By contrast, the service system in which the dirty worker operates is characterized by ambivalence toward the client, which manifests itself in terms of token and symbolic services funded at levels inadequate to need and demand. According to the latter model, the latent, if not manifest, service emphasis is punitive rather than humanitarian, focusing on social control as opposed to social integration and social justice.

There is some truth associated with each of these models. Which model, or what aspects of either model, operates in given situations is empirically problematic. The following chapters address the usefulness of such representations of contemporary public service workers and, by implication, the welfare system in which they operate.

Another issue represented in the literature on social welfare is how service provision may differ between private and public agencies (Rein, 1980). Private agencies in the abstract are characterized by small client domains and the ability to decide whom to serve. Services are well-defined and adequately funded for the range of clientele. Services are relatively holistic and are likely to result in a good prognosis for the recipient, who tends to be of middle-class status.

Public agencies, in contrast, serve large client domains and tend not to have organizational control over choice of clients. Services provided by public agencies are vaguely defined and under-funded. Further, the services offered are typically concerned only with a single aspect of the client's circumstances. These services are less likely than their private counterparts to result in problem resolution because of their fragmented nature and the more intractable problems of typically lower-income beneficiaries. While the distinction between these two types of organizations becomes blurred as greater numbers of private organizations seek public funding (e.g., Netting, 1982), they are useful models nevertheless. This book is concerned with how and to what extent the typical characteristics of public agencies influence the everyday work experiences of their service personnel.

A third theme found in social welfare literature is a concern with the phenomenon popularly labelled *burnout*. Studies typically have found that moderate to high levels of stress are characteristic of contemporary social service work, especially in public service organizations. To summarize briefly, it is argued in the burnout literature that inadequacies in service workers' approaches to their work and in the structure and climate of the service organization contribute to emotional exhaustion by service providers, i.e., they become burned out. In turn, service providers cope with such feelings through depersonalization and labelling of the client, reduced work performance, absenteeism, and job turnover. One of the major emphases of this book is to supplement and critique the available work on burnout by looking to broader areas for its causes.

The everyday world of service work will be looked at in some detail, focusing on types of stresses that are manifest in the daily routines of public service workers. The interviews with service providers in aging provide empirical documentation of their troubles and firsthand descriptions of typical situations. In each of the following sections, references to the literature in other human services is provided in order to link the respondents' experiences to other welfare undertakings. These references reinforce the claim that the experiences of the respondents are not unique; rather, they have counterparts across various public social services. Why this is so becomes clear in Chapters 3 and 4.

Turning now to the concerns of the respondents, four major areas of complaint in providing human services were found: (1) certain client characteristics that are sources of irritation and frustration; (2) problems with the service agency itself; (3) lack of resources to do an adequate job; and (4) mandates, rules, and regulations pertaining to services that hinder the performance of one's work.

CLIENT CHARACTERISTICS

The majority of the service providers interviewed had either taken their present positions because of their interest in helping people or had found great satisfaction, once on the job, from the opportunity to help others. A number of them entered their work with the ethic of altruism. Typical of this orientation are their responses to the question of how one decides to do this kind of work. Common answers were variations on these statements: "I had an interest in people in general," or "I enjoyed working with the elderly." Similarly, in response to a question about work rewards and satisfactions, it was common to hear the following remarks:

> [Y]ou kind of get a sense of plugging into something important when you can help somebody else at a critical time in his life. . . .
>
> I enjoy the face-to-face contact. I enjoy the idea of improving peoples' economic state, especially with times being as awful as they are. . . .
>
> The rewards are [both] tangible and intangible: the feeling of satisfaction I

get from working with senior citizens who, to a very great degree, are extremely grateful for any little thing or attention that you give them.

Such altruistic orientations are not unique to individuals working in services to the aging. Indeed, a study of reasons for choosing social work as a profession found that most social workers listed "working with people" as a prime motivator (Pins, 1963). Similarly, a recent study of public school teachers in New York (Fiske, 1982) reported that nearly two-thirds of all respondents said that helping or motivating children was what they like most about being a teacher.

Yet, it is also common to hear complaints by service providers about the clients with whom they work. Complaints that are related to client characteristics can be grouped into three major categories: (1) client dependencies; (2) lack of control over the provider-client relationship; and (3) lack of visible success in the service enterprise.

Client Dependencies

The very nature of service work means serving clients. In fact, social welfare policies frequently function to make clients dependent upon service providers in an ongoing way. Client passivity and dependence can make the provider's interaction with the client easier and validate the need for the service provider (Maslach, 1978). Nevertheless, one major source of frustration and dissatisfaction reported by a number of our respondents, as well as by providers of health care (Groves, 1978) and therapeutic services (Larson et al., 1978), is unnecessary dependency by service recipients. The interviewers perceive untoward dependency as the unwillingness of clients to do for themselves what they seem capable of doing.

This vexation was expressed vividly by several of the interviewees:

> I just don't feel that the elderly [are] as involved [in service efforts] as they ought to be, and . . . I don't feel that they . . . really advocate for themselves in terms of what they want. Many times they will say, "Why, y'all know what we need and what we want. You just go on and plan this program."

> There are people who call a hundred times and ask us the number for a senior center when I know they have the booklet right in front of them,

but they are just too lazy to pick it up and look it up. So they call us, as if all we have to do in the world is to answer simple questions.

I have one particular [participant] who is just a little older than I am, and I want to tell him, "If you'd get out and walk a little bit, exercise a little bit, you could do about as much work as I'm doing." But he enjoys the sympathy, and you have to be very careful that you don't sympathize with him. . . .

Demands such as these are perceived as illegitimate. They tax the time and energy of the worker, who is thrust into the situation of being fully responsible for the outcome of service efforts. As seen later in this chapter, workers feel a keen sense of a lack of time to accomplish all that must be done; client dependency contributes significantly to such a perception. In addition, Zerubavel (1976) argues that social respect is related to the degree to which others refrain from wasting one's time. Insofar as workers believe that certain clients waste their time, they may also sense disrespect from them.

Lack of control

Another client-related source of stress and dissatisfaction is the worker's lack of control over the provider-client role relationship (*see* Lipsky, 1980). This frustration has been reported for child welfare workers (Wasserman, 1970), therapists (Larson et al., 1978), police (Maslach and Jackson, 1978; Westley, 1953), public interest group employees (Bryan, 1981), those involved in patient care (Maslach, 1979; Wilson, 1963), and emergency room personnel (Roth, 1972), as well as for interviewees working in services for the aging. Lack of control takes two characteristic forms with the respondents, either lack of control over the expectations of the provider-client relationship or lack of control over the timing of that relationship.

Lack of control over expectations involves the inability of the provider to prevail in defining the extent of service to be rendered (*see* Maslach, 1978; Sarbin and Allen, 1968) and to shape the client's demeanor accordingly. As Roth (1972:845) notes, "Every worker has a notion of what demands are appropriate to his position. When demands fall outside that boundary, he feels that the claim is illegitimate." This frustration is closely linked to client dependencies, but it is not always expressed in that form.

One particular type of client demeanor related to lack of provider control is client treatment of the provider as a servant. According to one of the interviewees:

One of the surprises that really floored me [about this work]...is the demanding nature of some of the senior citizens..., the attitude [they have] that [a service] is owed to them.

Another service worker commented:

[Some] people won't accept no for an answer. [Sometimes] there is nothing I can do—there really isn't anything—or they have a request that just can't be filled, and they start hasseling you. I end up feeling like I wish [they'd] hang up the phone, leave me alone. Generally they are the people who are in the mood to harrass you.

Another form of lack of control relates to the timing of the client-provider role relationship. Situations that do not allow the worker to decide the timing of service provision are epitomized by the client emergency. This is a situation in which the client presents a need as urgent, even life threatening; consequently, it forces workers to reorganize their tasks (*see* Lipsky, 1980). Roth's study (1972) of hospital emergency room (ER) services provides the literal illustration of this point. A persistent complaint among his ER respondents was rampant public abuse of the ER. In other words, they perceived most of the cases as too minor to warrant ER usage.

The type of client emergency that causes frustration is illustrated in this vignette:

Sometimes [clients] tell you stories. Sometimes they call in and claim they are half-dead.... [O]nce we had a referral [in which] someone had really convinced the person on the phone that they were really in dire need of a meal.... So I went out to do the referral. I rang the doorbell, ... and I was thinking, "Wow, this lady is really sick. It's taking her a long time to come to the door." I walked to the side ... to see if I could see in the window or anything. So up comes this lady storming through the back of the yard. I was thinking that she was a neighbor there to help. It couldn't be anything else. I mean, she was physically fit! This lady had been down in her garage or somewhere in the house ... and she was covered with this wet paint.... So she comes up, and when I tell her who I am, then she gets all slumpy-shouldered and everything, and I've never been so knocked off my feet before in my life. And then I found out that this is, she's the one, the client! . . . I guess because people are in hot water, they think they need to lie, but I would rather hear the truth.

However, if the client had told the truth in this case, it is not likely that she would have received a quick response, if any service at all. What is at stake in situations such as this is the ability to control definitions of the situation; these definitions, in turn, are directly related to the allocation of worker time and energy. When workers are unable to exercise such control, work frustrations and discontents are likely to emerge.

A third form of lack of control that characterizes public service agencies and their workers is the issue of which clients will be served (Rein, 1980; Maslach, 1978; Roth, 1972). As argued in Chapter 5, politicians are not concerned so much with who is served as with how many are served. Therefore, policies may provide few if any directives or guidelines for service providers in the selection of service beneficiaries. Discretion emerges informally, however (Peyrot, 1982; Street et al., 1979; Zimmerman, 1969; Roth, 1972; Scott, 1967a), with advantage accruing to clients deemed morally acceptable from the provider's standpoint (Lipsky, 1980; Mennerick, 1974; Becker, 1952; Bucher and Schatzman, 1962; Bittner 1967; Chalfant and Kurtz, 1972; Willie, 1960). Nevertheless, staff frustration derives from the lack of formal authority to manage client characteristics.

Lack of Success

A third client-centered issue that causes frustration or dissatisfaction is lack of visible client successes. It should be noted first that service providers are readily forthcoming in describing individual clients whose situations have improved and in acknowledging client responsiveness and appreciation. As two of the interviewees related:

A senior citizen might come in and bring you a tomato and say, "Gee, I love you," or "Gee, I appreciate what you helped me with." . . . They are very touch-oriented people. Many of them will let you know they care through a hug or praise or defending you if they feel like that's necessary.

[I have highly positive feelings toward my clients] when the people with their eyes, with their lips, with their smiles, show us the expression of their appreciation for what we're trying to do and for making [each day] a little bit more happy for them to go through.

Nevertheless, Maslach (1978:116) points out:

Staff people often feel that their successes go away but that their failures keep coming back to haunt them and provide constant visible proof that they are incompetent and make mistakes.

The reappearance of unsuccessful clients is an empirical indicator of lack of success; so also is negative feedback from one's clients. As one respondent noted, "[T]here are people who, no matter what you do for them, are always complaining." According to Maslach (1978), clients are not socialized to provide the service worker with positive feedback; rather, they typically obtain what they need through complaints. In addition, certain clients have chronic conditions; hope for success is unrealistic, and service providers merely undertake efforts for client maintenance rather than improvement.

Work in the field of aging, especially in settings that serve ill and declining elders, can be characterized by disappointments due to lack of visible success. Such disappointments are also documented for workers in mental health settings (Pines and Maslach, 1978) and in hospitals (Maslach, 1979). One of the interviewees commented on these circumstances in a particularly poignant way:

[O]ne of the things . . . that kind of bothers me [is that] I get close to people and [I] realize that in a couple of years they are not going to be around. You don't think about that too often until you have been here a few years, and it starts to happen. I guess it kind of leaves a hole in your daily lifestyle. When a person that you see day by day is no longer there, there is an emptiness there that you sort of have to cope with. That is a special problem in working with the elderly—when you do open yourself and be vulnerable to people and do take them in as your friends, then you kind of hurt when they are no longer there.

In later pages it is argued that, with the exception of inevitable biological decline and terminal illness, clients' lack of success is traceable at least in part to the very structure of the welfare system and the policies that govern it. The issue of lack of client success is closely related to the complaints of lack of time and funding for services, which are explored shortly.

In sum, contrary to the model of service work as relatively autonomous and offering assistance to motivated recipients, the picture that emerges portrays the service worker as a captive of client demands that may or may not be perceived as legitimate. Further, the client is not necessarily grateful for what is received; indeed, the client may treat the worker as a servant and demand certain benefits and attention. The service role holds out no guarantee that client successes will outnumber failures; in fact, the system is structured to recycle the unsuccessful for further provider attention. Finally, the service system appears less than equally accessible to clients; rather, individuals who are demanding or who embellish their situations with the greatest sense of urgency are most likely to receive service provider attention.

AGENCY PROBLEMS

A second major source of work dissatisfaction for service providers concerns issues of the service organization itself: (1) job ambiguity, or lack of job specificity and program structure and (2) differing perspectives about the service enterprise at various levels of the work organization.

Job Ambiguity

Two forms of job ambiguity, lack of job specificity and program structure, are sources of frustration for a large number of the individuals interviewed. The following situations are illustrative of the lack of specificity in their work:

> At the time I was interviewed for the job, there was a job description, or job responsibilities or duties, however you want to term it, that was ... in fine detail, ... and after joining the organization, I found ... the way it was described to me ... was about as far from the product I got into as you could possibly get into.

> [M]y job description says that I am to ... administer this program, to be innovative and creative, but that's not what it is, ... because [someone else] does that. I think we should sit down sometime and get a clear understanding of who is to do what.

[This job] has involved a lot of different kinds of things that I didn't know would be involved. For instance, when I first started working here and we were setting up priorities of things that needed to be done, there were eight number one priorities.... I think [it is] sometimes difficult to decide..., "Which one of these things am I going to work on now?"

The programs that workers operate may be riddled with ambiguities, too:

[W]hen I got here, there was not a whole lot of structure for me to follow, and... there are still... questions about what this particular service is supposed to do.... I did expect to have more structure for the program itself, which I didn't get. We had to sort of forge that for ourselves....

This quotation describes ambiguity within a service agency; programming ambiguity is also manifested in relationships between agencies:

We had a contract... to provide the meals to homebound people, and part of what's expected is social services. I have trouble deciding where... we leave off in providing social services, and where... other agencies pick up. I mean, we can't be a case manager for every client that gets a meal from our agency. We aren't equipped to do that; we aren't staffed to do that.... And sometimes I get the impression that that's what we are really expected to do. Yet we are not really funded to do that.

Ambiguity surrounding one's work is a common source of stress in many types of work organizations (Gross, 1970; French and Caplan, 1972; Cherniss, 1978). In the human services it is reported in public interest work (Bryan, 1981), police work (Maslach and Jackson, 1979), and nursing (Helmer, 1982), in addition to being reported by the workers in aging services. Ambiguity is further exacerbated when staff fail to receive supervision or feedback about their work from administrators, supervisors, or colleagues (e.g., Billingsley et al., 1966; Pines and Kafry, 1978). Parenthetically, public agency administrators report role ambiguity in their jobs, too (Rogers and Molnar, 1976). While job ambiguity can result from inappropriate management styles within agencies, it is argued in later chapters that ambiguity is inherent in the welfare policies that service workers implement. Thus, it is not surprising that service personnel find ambiguity a source of frustration.

Differing Perspectives

Another source of agency-centered work dissatisfaction derives from the different vantage points of individuals at various levels of social service organizations (*see* Lipsky, 1980). A number of service providers report becoming frustrated when administrators deny their requests for additional resources or alterations in programming activities:

> I've had people say, "Why is it that we cannot get . . . the top [administrators] to deal with certain things better?" And I think it's because they are not in direct services. They do not really know what is going on. Sometimes we have some problems with . . . things that we want to purchase, and you think sometimes the money is coming out of that person's pocket rather than from a program. It can be frustrating when we come up with some goals . . . and someone else farther up will say, "You can't do that." [There's] a lack of understanding [by those higher up] of what's going on day to day with the clients; [they're just] looking at it from a management standpoint.

> [W]e don't have too much control over contracts and budgets and negotiating. That at times is very frustrating because we are working with the program daily, and we know what the needs are. We know what it takes to operate the program effectively. . . . [W]e have input into what goes into the contract, but by the time the contract finally comes back to us, it's been changed and mutilated.

Constraints from above are also a source of discontent for child protective service workers (Billingsley et al., 1966), workers in prerelease programs for adult offenders (Sarata and Reppucci, 1975), and police (Maslach and Jackson, 1979). This complaint converges with complaints of lack of participation in agency decision making (e.g., French and Caplan, 1972) and lack of agency support (Pines and Kafry, 1978; Fiske, 1982) to wrest a sense of control from service workers. Often these workers overlook the fact that agency administrators also labor under constraints from above. This is evident in the following statement of a former agency director:

> Functioning in a position between policymakers, regulation-enforcers, funding sources, and staff was a difficult position, particularly where line staff were concerned. [These were] people who daily come into contact with older people and are quite knowledgeable about and concerned about the daily needs of those older people, and unable many times to respond positively to those needs and not understanding why they couldn't. [Being in] that kind of position was tension-producing.

It is possible that the problems created by differing orientations within an agency are partly due to the managerial style. However, it is maintained later that the difficulties of service work emanating from different vantage points are inherent in the structure of service work.

In sum, service workers, far from being autonomous in their jobs, experience definite constraints on what they do. They must negotiate their roles from both the demands made by their clients and the constraints imposed by their administrators. What autonomy exists in the public agency derives as much from lack of clarity about what should be done as it does from an accepted norm of independence and discretion. Workers report a service system characterized by ambiguity surrounding who should serve whom in what way. This depiction is far from the ideal of the systemic integration of services sought by service networks.

LACK OF RESOURCES

A third source of work dissatisfactions for service providers is the lack of resources for proper and timely execution of their job responsibilities (*see* Lipsky, 1980). The particular resources the interviewees mentioned as being in short supply are worker time and program funding.

Lack of Time

The perceived lack of time is related to two interdependent provider responsibilities: case load management and paperwork administration. Small caseloads requiring intensive client interaction, large caseloads, or a combination of caseload and paperwork duties, create time problems. Providers maintain that there is simply not enough time in their workday to perform all of the tasks expected of them. These situations are exacerbated by the fact that most workers' jobs have no clear boundaries, despite job titles or job descriptions that state otherwise. Consequently, it is not surprising that one service provider saw herself as an "overstretched rubber band"; another described herself as "a rag doll with half the stuffing gone" ("Career Burnout," 1980:5).

The following remarks offer a detailed look at how time becomes a problem in service work:

> [T]o meet all the clients on the program, that's a big task for one person. We have about 200 clients [for] which I'm the primary provider. I think that's an unrealistic goal because they need so much, and stretching one person too thin really doesn't get that much done. When you're stretching, you have to take care of referrals, you have to take care of clients, you have to take care of emergency cases, and [you have to] work with some in terms of social services. In working with social services, sometimes the problems are so complex until it takes a long time just working with one individual. ... I am solely [responsible for doing all of that] because there's nobody else to do it. .... Everything is needed right now, and we just don't have the staff to take care of the needs of the homebound, because it's like one-to-one relationships. That means you have to go out to their house, and first you've got to find it, and then you've got to sit and talk. They're lonely; you can understand that, and they really want to talk. And you might sit there for an hour, an hour and a half, and then finally you get to the problem.

Heavy case loads, either in qualitative or quantitative terms, impair satisfactory work performance and reduce the likelihood of client success. The complaint of excessive caseloads, and, consequently, of the lack of time for their proper management, has also been registered in public assistance programs (Scott, 1969), legal services (Maslach and Jackson, 1978), child care (Maslach and Pines, 1977), therapy (Larson et al., 1978), mental health (Pines and Maslach, 1978), and public health nursing (Helmer, 1982). Lack of time is likely to be most acute among service providers who are highly dedicated to the personal aspects of the provider-client relationship (Freudenberger, 1974; Cherniss, 1978; Marks, 1979), who have an inability to say no to additional caseload demands (Larson et al., 1978; Bryan, 1981), whose orientation to clients is one of continuous coverage (Zerubavel, 1979b) or high protectiveness (LaRossa and LaRossa, 1981), and who work with individuals who are otherwise isolated from interpersonal contacts. In the latter case the service provider becomes a major agent of social integration, and client requests can expand indefinitely. Relating to one's clients in personalized, sympathetic, or holistic ways becomes dysfunctional with regard to time and work demands on the service provider (Zimmerman, 1969; Street et al., 1980; Lipsky, 1980).

A few service providers compensate for lack of time by allowing themselves to be accessible to clients beyond regular work hours. These are workers who choose to live in what Glasser (1976) calls a small world, that is, a world where there is singular overcommitment to a particular activity. One respondent described her commitment:

> I am . . . classified as a part-time worker, and my hours are from nine to three, but, of course, you can't keep those hours as a matter of routine because the problems come in maybe at 6:00 at night or maybe at 7:00 in the morning. So, I work as I am called. . . . [T]ime is meaningless to a lot of my participants who are homebound, and I don't object at all to their calling me at 11:00 at night if they can't sleep or something like that. . . .

A second worker noted, "When I'm called at home at 6:00 in the morning or at 8:00 at night, . . . I feel like [my work] is very important."

For some providers, being perpetually on call provides ego gratification and status enhancement (Sieber, 1974); for others it leads to further complaints about their job. Frustration over the lack of time-out from work responsibilities is not peculiar to workers in aging; it is reported as well in studies of police (Maslach and Jackson, 1979), mental health service providers (Pines and Maslach, 1978), and general social service workers (Pines and Kafry, 1978). These workers feel that there are no respected boundaries between their work and private life and that they have no private time for themselves (Zerubavel, 1979a). One service worker characterized herself as "a checking account with frequent withdrawals and no deposits" ("Career Burnout," 1980:5).

While one's time seems inadequate for meeting client needs, the intrusion of paperwork further diminishes the amount of time for service provision. Frustrations over paperwork are described later under "Mandates, Rules, and Regulations." For now it is sufficient to note that paperwork demands are believed to contribute significantly to lack of time for one's clients.

While lack of time is a common complaint among service providers, it must also be recognized that the claim "I don't have time" is a useful account for avoiding tasks that workers accord low priority (Marks, 1977; Lyman and Scott, 1970). Some workers use lack of time as an occupationally honorable excuse to avoid or decrease encounters with troublesome clients, deflect requests from coworkers, or seek respite from personalized contacts by devoting their time to the demands of paperwork (Toren, 1969; Wasserman, 1971).

Lack of Funding

Lack of funds is another major complaint of social service personnel. Service workers feel that more staff would provide needed relief from the stresses of their heavy work loads. However, they recognize that the employment of additional staff requires additional funds that are not likely to be available.

If additional funds were available, they could also be employed to bolster programming efforts. Limited programming is another source of discontent. One worker noted, "[It] is very disheartening because I have to tell the person, 'I'm sorry. There is nothing we can do.'" A second provider described how lack of funding demands arbitrary limitations on services:

> [It is frustrating when you see] a person living in his home that has too much money to qualify for a particular program, but just barely, and it doesn't counterbalance the inflationary process on that person. You see him struggling, and he can't be eligible for the service because of that one eligibility requirement. It seems like there are people out there who just don't fit into this category or that category, so they just can't be serviced. There is just not enough time, money, or people available to do the servicing.

Still a third respondent detailed the juggling act that occurs with limited funds available for programs:

> [The 126 meals served] are not even a drop in the bucket. So sometimes you're even forced, if a person is even a little bit better, to take them off the program. . . . They really could stay on the program, but you've got somebody else out there who's in worse shape than he is. It's just sad. We're fighting over crumbs.

Providers tend to see their particular program or activity as being the most underfunded. For example, transportation coordinators and drivers see the need for more drivers and vans as a top priority, while nutritionists believe that funds should be transferred from activities such as recreation to nutritional services. This results from seeing unmet needs occurring within one's own jurisdiction, from a sense of tunnel vision related to one's specialization (Avant and Dressel, 1980), and from the likelihood that no programs are funded at a level that meets demands. The outcome of such tunnel vision can be intraagency rivalry for the funds that are available or, as seen in an earlier section, a belief that administrators are overly protective of agency funds.

There is evidence to reinforce the claims of workers in aging that the lack of resources precludes adequate job performance. A report from the Subcommittee on Human Services of the United States House of Representatives Select Committee on Aging (1980) cites the following statistics about the population with whom the interviewees work:

> Overall, 73 percent of our elder population is currently in need of some kind of help; 12 percent are receiving all the help they need, but a whopping 61 percent are not.... [W]e are not responding to three out of every five elders in America....

Additional evidence indicates that the severest inadequacies of funds and staff are found in rural areas (Nelson, 1980).

In sum, the related issues of lack of time, staff, and money provide ongoing sources of personal frustration, role stress, and work dissatisfaction for service providers. This picture is in stark contrast to the ideal of a comprehensive service system outlined at the beginning of the chapter.

The blame for such frustrations has frequently been placed on the individual worker or the particular service agency. Workers' inabilities to manage time wisely, to say no to demands of clients and coworkers, and to provide for their own private time have been viewed as major sources of the problem of lack of time. At the agency level, improper management of staff time, and waste and abuse of public funds have been the accusations associated with lack of time and lack of funds, respectively. It will be argued later, however, that larger contributors to inadequate resources have been overlooked. These include cultural expectations demanding worker commitment, overly ambitious welfare policies, and the ambivalence of politicians and the general public toward social welfare activities.

MANDATES, RULES, AND REGULATIONS

A fourth source of worker dissatisfaction is the myriad of rules, regulations, and mandates under which programming operates and the paperwork necessary to document compliance with these procedures.

Many decisions about program implementation are handed down from the federal level, resulting in constraints on decision making about local programming. One former agency administrator described the situation as follows:

> In aging there are policies that are made at the national level that I suppose are based on national data, not local data. My opinion has been that national data can sometimes present a priority that is not at the local level. But because of priorities and policies set at the national level related to funding, it's impossible to use that funding for anything except the priority that has been set or the particular service that has been identified. . . . Our agency was dependent upon federal, state, and local public money, and there were always strings attached to those funding sources: regulations that we had to deal with, guidelines that had to be recognized, policies that were developed at some other level that determined the directions. [A] primary drawback was . . . not having the flexibility with the funding that would enable us to go in different directions.

For direct service providers, guidelines can cause confusion and frustration. One respondent remarked, for example, "There were several times that we wanted to help somebody in a certain area of the city, and we weren't supposed to because they didn't live in the right neighborhood." Another respondent who works in a senior center offered the following illustration of this complaint:

> [W]e were allocated [funds for] 35 people, but I only have 25 coming, so I have 10 extra slots for people. Then I get a team in that builds up interest here, and they whip [attendance] up to 40. But by that time our allotment is cut back because our average is only 25. . . . It just seems like things don't jell all at the same time. When the need is there, you don't always have the programs and money . . . to meet that need, and when you don't have the need, you have plenty of [resources].

Such frustrations have led service workers to characterize themselves as "meeting a brick wall" or "always finding Dead End signs" ("Career Burnout," 1980:5).

The implication of these comments is that greater discretion should be allowed at the local level for priority setting and resource allocation. The same themes were widely articulated by national aging organizations during testimony on the 1978 reauthorization of the Older Americans Act (Estes and Gerard, n.d.). They are at the heart of the rhetoric of the Reagan administration's argument for returning social welfare functions to the states. It should be noted, however, that Rogers and Molnar's (1976) study of 110 top-level administrators of public county-level offices found that the opportunity for local autonomy was significantly related to role conflict for agency administrators. Trade-offs appear to be involved in achieving local decision-making authority for federal funds.

The additional complaint of constantly changing mandates, rules, and regulations has been registered by some service providers, most notably public child welfare workers (Wasserman, 1971; Street et al., 1979). For these workers,

> public assistance policies and practices are in almost perpetual flux, reflecting the complex permutations of the phasings of federal, state, county, [and] local administrative fiscal processes, the vagaries of political decisions, pressures, cycles of virtue and terror, and local grassroots demands, and the organizational disarray induced by shifts in caseload size, turnover of employees, and so on. . . . [P]olicies are in perpetual fluidity from office to office and from day to day. (Street et al., 1979:40)

Such confusion enhances the ambiguity of agency work and inevitably produces low morale among workers who must execute their tasks amidst the confusion.

Finally, a large number of respondents complained about the paperwork accompanying mandates, rules, and regulations. Here are some of the comments they made:

> There is a lot of paperwork involved in this job. . . . There is a lot of accountability, and I'm not sure that it is worth all the effort that we put into it. It just takes away a lot of my time and energy that I need to be doing other things with the [clients]. If I have to record every single thing that I do, I would not have time to do it. . . . Obviously there is a balance, and obviously you can't have programs unless you can verify that they are

doing something to the funding sources. That's understandable. But there's a point where it gets to be out of control and off balance.

Title XX [of the Social Security Act] requires a lot of time, a lot of work. [T]hey sent out a questionnaire to find out how much time we spend working on monthly reports. . . . There are so many things we could be doing for the client while we're having to report to someone on units [of service].

There are data available beyond that provided by the interviewees to document their plight and to corroborate their perceptions about the heavy load of paperwork. A report for the United States Senate Special Committee on Aging (Estes and Noble, 1978:8) noted the large amount of paperwork required in implementing the Older Americans Act, through which the interviewees' agencies are funded. The report stated:

The Older Americans Act reporting system for Titles III and VII [combined. in later OAA amendments] alone annually amasses more than 15,000 million items of data dealing with basic contract compliance, at an annual cost exceeding $1 million just for reproducing the forms and copying the reports for minimum mandated distribution. . . . Since neither the work effort required to fill out this paper nor the program costs due to staff time lost are calculated in such estimates of paperwork costs, the basic [paperwork costs] represent only the tip of the iceberg relative to the actual costs of maintaining the paper flow.

These data alone are startling. In addition, it should be realized that they represent the paperwork requirements for only a single source of program funding. The programs with which the interviewees are associated receive funding from numerous other sources as well (e.g., Title XX, HUD, Medicaid, state and local public revenues, and private donations and grants), all of which have their own specialized reporting systems. It is not surprising that complaints exist across publicly funded human service specializations about the inordinate amounts of paperwork associated with their funding (Fiske, 1982; Matthews, 1982; Scott, 1969; Cherniss, 1978; Wasserman, 1971).

Matthews's (1982) study of a transportation service for the elderly vividly demonstrates how paperwork becomes a dominant activity once external funding is obtained. The case on which she reports is the evolution of a cooperative transportation system into a complex agency function funded through several sources. Once the agency took over the system, drivers were required to begin spending over an hour per day on paperwork to enable proper billing of the funding sources and insure agency accountability to the funders. The original system, by contrast, had been one that only required the driver to collect money from passengers and relay it to a single fund controlled by a transportation cooperative.

In short, the picture of public service work that emerges from the data is one of constraints from above that in whole or in part dictate who shall be served, in what manner, by whom, under what conditions, and for what length of time. Accompanying such directives are demands for accountability that erode workers' time and energies for direct service provision. The strictly regulated aspects of service work are consistent with the dirty worker model of service provision presented earlier. Dirty work is epitomized by circumstances such as withholding service from clients who do not fall into applicable categories, withdrawing services that meet political misfortune, and treating service recipients as piecemeal problems because comprehensive service orientations are neither fiscally nor politically feasible (*see* Chapter 5).

CONSEQUENCES OF WORKER DISSATISFACTIONS

The foregoing has highlighted a number of dissatisfactions that characterize service work. Are these dissatisfactions significant? In other words, do they adversely affect service workers, their clients, the service agency, or other social systems of which the service worker is a part? If so, then perhaps intervention strategies are in order.

The stresses that service workers encounter in their daily work can have significant impact on their job attitudes, job performance, and personal health. With regard to job attitudes, work stresses take their toll in increased incidences of apathy, cynicism, loss of idealism, feelings of helplessness and hopelessness, and generally low morale. Job performance is affected by lack of initiative, loss of concern for clients, the ritualistic application of rules, increased absenteeism, increasingly critical attitudes toward coworkers, and declining motivation to cooperate with others in work activities. Finally, the service workers' physical health can be impacted through increased use of alcohol or drugs or through an increased vulnerability to disease that accompanies feelings of physical and emotional exhaustion (e.g., Fiske, 1982; Edelwich, 1980; Cherniss, 1978, 1980b; Maslach, 1976, 1979; Maslach and Jackson, 1978, 1979). At the extreme is the possibility of suicide, the rates of which are disproportionately high for police, medical doctors, and psychiatrists.

Insofar as service providers utilize physical or emotional withdrawal as a means of coping with their work discontents, the service recipient is likely to be affected. Numerous studies have highlighted dissatisfied or burned out workers' loss of concern for the client. This loss of concern is manifested in ways such as depersonalization of the provider-client relationship, physical detachment from the client, distrust or dislike of the client, scapegoating of the client for work-related problems, the labelling and stereotyping of recipients, and a lack of sympathy and respect for them (Edelwich, 1980; Mennerick, 1974; Cherniss, 1978; Maslach, 1976, 1978, 1979; Roth, 1972; Maslach and Jackson, 1978, 1979). These orientations, in turn, can generate dissatisfactions and regressive behaviors by clients (e.g., Schwartz and Will, 1953; Stotland and Kobler, 1965; Sarata and Reppucci, 1974; Edelwich, 1980), or client stereotypes of the workers (Mennerick, 1974), thereby reinforcing the declining quality of the relationship.

The service agency is also affected by the symptoms or consequences of worker dissatisfactions. The agency is less able to pursue its goals efficiently or effectively when providers demonstrate loss of concern for clients, lowered morale and motivation, and increased absenteeism. In addition, workers' dissatisfactions can be contagious for other staff members, creating an even greater problem of employee morale. Dissatisfied workers may demonstrate lack of cooperation with fellow employees, making effective agency performance increasingly difficult. Finally, the moderately high turnover rate that characterizes public service work can create organizational discontinuities that may affect goal performance (Maslach, 1976, 1979; Cherniss, 1978, 1980b; Maslach and Jackson, 1978, 1979; Edelwich, 1980; Karger, 1981). On the other hand, turnover can contribute to the replacement of burned-out workers with fresher, more motivated personnel.

Immediate work relationships are not the only areas affected by dissatisfied public service workers. It also appears that the family of the service worker serves as a shock absorber for the stress that the worker carries home. Researchers have found that stressed or alienated workers may experience marital conflict resulting from such factors as their unwillingness to talk about their work situation at home, their use of alcohol or drugs to cope, their ongoing accessibility to work peers beyond normal working hours, or the depression or irritability that accompanies exhaustion (Maslach, 1976; Maslach and Jackson, 1979). Relationships with children may suffer from similar influences as well (Cherniss, 1980b).

For all of these reasons it is important to be concerned with both the sources and the consequences of service worker discontents. It will become clear as this book unfolds, in fact, that these stresses and workers' responses to them have ramifications throughout the social welfare system. In looking at what others have said regarding the sources of worker conflicts and stresses, it becomes clear that only part of the picture has been painted.

WHO'S TO BLAME?

Interest in the manifestations, causes, and treatment of stresses in the human services has accelerated since the seminal article by Freudenberger in 1974 on the plight of committed but burned-out mental health workers. The bulk of publications on service worker stresses focuses on the micro-systems in which the service worker operates. (The exceptions are Cherniss [1980b] and Karger [1981].) Thus, social psychological, organizational, and administrative orientations to service worker stresses dominate the literature. Investigators have focused on individual behaviors and personalities and on characteristics of the work setting to determine what causes workers' problems and, therefore, where interventions for the alleviation of these problems should be directed. What are the conclusions of these studies? In this chapter only stressors are highlighted; Chapter 5 reviews corresponding recommendations for intervention.

From a social psychological perspective, the causes of work stresses are either intrapersonal or interpersonal. The intrapersonal orientation suggests a number of attitudes, needs, and work habits of the service provider that lead to work stress, dissatisfaction, and burnout. These include such factors as the inability to say no to additional responsibility, an intense work style (workaholism), an inability to separate one's work and personal life, a heightened sense of idealism and commitment, and low coping skills (Bryan, 1981; Edelwich, 1980; Maslach, 1978; Larson et al., 1978; Maslach and Jackson, 1979; Cherniss, 1978; Freudenberger, 1974).

Interpersonal causes of stress refer to relationships either with clients or coworkers. Client relationships are likely to be troublesome when they are characterized by the provider's strong desire to be liked and accepted, the provider's overidentification with the clients' problems, a focus on negative situations and negative feedback, and differential expectations about the role relationship (Maslach, 1978; Cherniss, 1978; Sarbin and Allen, 1968). In addition, relationships with coworkers are likely to be stressful when they are characterized by ambiguous lines of authority, lack of support and feedback, and structural and functional isolation (Cherniss, 1978; French and Caplan, 1972; Larson, et al., 1978; Pines and Maslach, 1978; Pines and Kafry, 1978).

From an organizational or an administrative perspective, causes of worker dissatisfactions revolve around the content of the work and working conditions. Specific characteristics of work in human services that are claimed to cause worker dissatisfaction include working with clients whose successful outcome is unlikely, having responsibility for the well-being of others, experiencing unpredictable crises, being unable to define worker success in a concrete way due to uncertainty and vagueness of expectations, and having to make quick decisions when information is not always available or clear-cut (Bryan, 1981; Sarbin and Allen, 1968; Maslach, 1979; Maslach and Jackson, 1979; French and Caplan 1972; Pines and Maslach, 1978).

Working conditions also generate discontent. These include high caseloads, long work hours, the lack of time-outs, an inordinate amount of time with paperwork rather than people, lack of participation in decision making, frustrations with administrators, bureaucratic inertia, lack of clear work direction or feedback, worker isolation, continual changes in rules and regulations, and low salaries (Edelwich, 1980; Larson et al., 1978; Billingsley, et al.,

1966; Cherniss, 1978; Maslach and Pines, 1977; Maslach and Jackson, 1978; Wasserman, 1971; Maslach, 1978; French and Caplan, 1972; Pines and Maslach, 1978).

In sum, social psychological and organizational studies suggest that the problems human service workers experience derive either from their own inadequate personalities or improper work orientations, inadequate relationships with clients or coworkers, the nature of their jobs, or their immediate work environment. However, the fact that service worker complaints are reproduced across agencies and client types and throughout worker levels indicates, alternatively, that the way in which the larger human service enterprise is structured may contribute to worker dissatisfactions. While standard social psychological and organizational variables may explain part of workers' difficulties, there is enough consistency across these variables to dictate further exploration of sources of discontent. Chapter 3 looks at the structure of contemporary public service work to ascertain how its inherent contradictions and conflicts contribute to service worker problems and social welfare failures. Then, Chapter 4 demonstrates how the larger environment of service work, which is characterized by political fragmentation and cultural and historical ambivalence, creates problems for providers. While others have argued variations of this broader orientation (e.g., Lubove, 1969; Zimmerman, 1969; Wasserman, 1971; Finch, 1976; Howe, 1980; Lipsky, 1980), it is a major point of this book to demonstrate how the inherent difficulties of the social welfare system get played out on a day-to-day basis, how service workers fail to understand larger sources of their work discontent, and how their day-to-day coping behaviors sum collectively into a perpetuation of the very problems that generated their original work dissatisfactions.

Chapter 3

THE STRUCTURE OF SERVICE WORK
Caught in the Middle

The structure of human service work is characterized by conflicts and contradictions that generate some of the problems detailed in the preceding chapter. This chapter demonstrates that human service providers are people caught in the middle; that is, they are located between various contradictory or conflicting imperatives of the social welfare enterprise. Consequently, the problems they experience are inevitable. At least part of the tensions of service work, then, derives from the structural arrangements of the occupation itself.

The broadest possible overview of public service work must take into account its functions in an advanced capitalist society. In brief, the task of the welfare system is to diminish the impact of unemployment and related problems on citizens displaced from the mainstream of the economy or lacking adequate access to other social institutions. Welfare assistance must be provided at a level that prevents massive unrest by the displaced (Piven and Cloward, 1971); at the same time it must not be so adequate that it reduces individuals' motivations to work.

Welfare assistance is unlikely to be provided at an adequate level due to the limited resources of the public sector. The inherently limited resources stem from two basic, but contradictory, functions of government: on the one hand, it functions to provide an environment fertile for economic production, the profits of which remain in the private sector; on the other hand, it is expected to handle the spillover of humanity displaced from the production process, but it has minimal private profit and limited public revenues with which to do that (O'Connor, 1973).

The tasks of public service workers are made difficult because of

40

these contradictory functions. The daily problems workers face are not typically expressed as difficulties stemming from the privatization of profit and the socialization of the costs of that profit making (O'Connor, 1973); nevertheless, many of them have their roots in these fundamental dynamics. In effect, service providers are caught in the middle of incompatible social forces operating in the larger society.

At the day-to-day, face-to-face level of social welfare, being caught in the middle takes on several different forms. The specific forms of contradictions and conflicts that are examined in this chapter include being caught in the middle between (a) client and organizational needs; (b) professional and organizational norms; and (c) professional and nonprofessional (i.e., "semiprofessional") occupational statuses. Each of these dilemmas is described, and the particular everyday problems they generate for service providers are noted.

CLIENT AND ORGANIZATIONAL NEEDS

Before it is possible to understand how service workers are caught in the middle between the needs of clients and the needs of the agency for which they work, or between what Warren (1967) calls output and input constituencies, respectively, it is necessary to spell out what the respective needs of these competing groups are.

The foremost need of the client is to obtain the benefits or services provided by an agency and its workers. The acquisition of these benefits or services implies the need for the worker's attention, time, and energy on behalf of the client. In turn, according to the Code of Ethics of the National Association of Social Workers passed in 1979, the primary responsibility of the service provider is to one's clients and to the service of their needs. Further, "[t]he social worker should avoid relationships or commitments that conflict with the interests of the clients" (Article II.F.4). The irony of this orientation is that most service workers are employed by agencies whose internal and external needs are in direct competition with the needs of the client (*see also* Lipsky, 1980).

On the other side, official decision makers and the lay public make dual demands on public agencies to serve the interests of the larger community in general and to protect the interests of the taxpayer in particular (Scott, 1969). Interests of the larger community revolve around the state functions already noted: reducing the likelihood of social unrest without undermining incentive for self-sufficiency. More specifically, political decision makers need agencies to provide them with at least symbolic successes to note to their constituents, if not concrete, quantifiable results of social improvement (Binstock and Levin, 1976). Within the organization these dictates get translated to the service provider as the need for public accountability, work efficiency, and measurable program effectiveness. In addition, organizational imperatives contribute the need for "institutional maintenance, protection, and growth" (Rein and Rabinovitz, 1978:313), regardless of an agency's impact on community problems. These agency needs are referred to as an "organizational secret" (Gouldner, 1963) because they may not be acknowledged as compelling forces behind agency decisions and actions, despite their prevalence and influence. In short, pressures exerted from the agency and those to whom it is accountable compete with client concerns for the priority attention and allegiance of social workers.

How do these competing demands get played out in the daily lives of human service providers? In part they become sources of service worker problems. Three of the four major areas of complaint described in Chapter 2 relate to contradictory or conflicting demands from clients and from agency administrators.

Agency Problems

Job ambiguity and conflicting perspectives are the two specific complaints the interviewees had about their service agencies. From the preceding discussion it can be seen that ambiguity is built into the structure of service work through the differing and possibly contradictory needs of clients and employers. For example, while clients may seek access to home-delivered meals, an employer may, for political or organizational reasons, urge workers to enhance enrollment in a congregate meals program instead.

How the worker should respond to a dilemma like this is unclear.

However, a strong argument can be made that many such situations will be resolved in the interests of the organization rather than in the interests of the client. The client is at a power disadvantage vis-à-vis the agency in the struggle for the attention and commitment of the service provider. As noted in the preceding chapter, while the client offers the rewards of approval and validation to the service worker, such positive feedback is not always forthcoming. Even if it were, the employing agency offers the far more valuable reward of employment. This imbalance of resources virtually guarantees that in important instances the worker will choose to meet the needs of supervisors and bosses before or above the needs of clients.

In addition, Levy (1970:170) notes that

> [t]he [welfare worker] can never be equal to the demands made on him by both the welfare bureaucracy and the hapless client.... [W]hile the requests of administrators and supervisors can be put off only for so long without sanctions being brought against the [worker], in most cases clients can be put off indefinitely.

Thus, power is not only an issue of the rewards offered by the competing groups; it is also a question of the severity of sanctions that each can impose. Clients do indeed have a varied bag of interpersonal tricks that can be troublesome for the service worker if they choose to employ them (e.g., Lipsky, 1980; Gubrium, 1975); however, it is much less significant to walk away from a client than it is from a job. In fact, it could be argued that clients are a virtually limitless commodity from which the choicest can be picked. On the other hand, the availability of service work jobs is a much rarer commodity that diminishes with fiscal retrenchment.

In sum, job ambiguity is predictable for service providers because they are caught in the middle of frequently conflicting demands from clients and their employing agency. Workers are most likely to resolve this dilemma on the side of the organization. In an empirical study of social workers, Billingsley (1964) found that his subjects were responsive foremost to the implementation of agency policies, next to the execution of professional social work standards, and last, to the actual meeting of clients' needs. This is a clear illustration of the client's lack of importance as a reference group (Lipsky, 1980) or power actor in relation to human service workers.

Following professional norms and being an advocate for clients is bound at times to put service workers in conflict with their own employer (Wasserman, 1971), a situation that is risky at best. In fact, one writer (Edelwich, 1980:Chap. 7) describes the subordination of client services to administrative and political requirements as a given of the service system. A second author (Scott, 1969) reports the situation of supervisors in a county public assistance agency attempting to deemphasize to caseworkers the importance of positive client reactions. The supervisors maintained that direct service providers should not rely on favorable feedback from clients as a source of work satisfaction precisely because being a good caseworker means having to generate negative responses from the client in order to fulfill the agency's dictates. Correspondingly, in a study of registered nurses, Alutto et al. (1971) found head nurses to be perceived as more important role definers for nurses working in a county hospital than are patients, even though nurses felt that the influence of patients should be increased. In contrast, nursing personnel in private facilities, specifically community and religious hospitals, perceived patients as primary in defining their roles. These findings suggest that important organizational or bureaucratic differences may exist between public and private health care facilities that impact directly on how service workers approach their jobs.

The second major agency problem the interviewees cited is conflicting perspectives between themselves and their supervisors and administrators. Differing priorities frequently emerged from debate over the allocation of agency resources. The previous discussion suggests that such conflict can be seen as virtually inevitable in a human service organization. Because of their respective positions in the service structure, providers seek the distribution of funds in accordance with perceived client needs; administrators, on the other hand, view the acquisition and distribution of funds as issues of organizational visibility, maintenance, or expansion and as issues of accountability to guidelines and regulations that they have been employed to oversee. According to Edelwich (1980:19), differing budgetary perspectives are typically resolved in the following manner:

More often than not, funds are allocated according to the political requirements of the institution, as perceived by top management, rather than
according to the needs of clients, as perceived by frontline workers who
provide direct services.

Matthews' (1982) observations of a transportation service system
for the elderly illustrate differing perspectives. From an administrative standpoint the ideal passenger is one who falls easily within
the boundaries of funding guidelines. On the other hand, the
ideal passenger as defined by the driver is one who is cooperative
and whose behavior is predictable. A further example is offered in
Latimore's (1979) study of a voluntary job placement agency. In
response to demands from funding sources for greater productivity,
job counselors began weeding out hard-to-place clients. This approach came at the expense of their altruistic work orientations
and their job's stated mission. Similarly, a memorandum to workers
in the Work Training Program in the State of Massachusetts Welfare Department ordered workers to cease their attempts to match
welfare recipients with jobs suitable to their skills and background
and refer them instead to any employment available. This mandate resulted from the agency's poor performance statistics in job
placement (Black, 1982).

While providers are caught in the middle between clients and
employers, agency administrators are also caught in the middle.
They are located between their workers, to whom they might wish
to respond favorably, and politicians, bureaucrats, and funding
sources, whose dictates might not enable them to do so. Yet, it is
frequently difficult for providers to understand that their superiors are caught in the middle as well. For example, a recent
attempt was made by home care workers in Massachusetts to
unionize against their supervisors. However, organizers overlooked
the fact that the supervisors were powerless to respond to certain
demands because they themselves were constrained by dictates of
the State Department of Elder Affairs. Further evidence of constraints on administrators derives from a study of mental health
agencies by Dehlinger and Perlman (1978). These authors cite
control by external institutions in such agency issues as staff
assignments, organizational layoffs, and funding.

Lack of Resources

Service workers' concern over lack of time is related in part to the conflicting demands of clients and administrators. The worker's dilemma is manifest most clearly around the issue of paperwork. Paperwork is a function that contributes to agency accountability; at the same time its performance eats into hours that service workers feel would be better spent with clients. Indeed, service providers believe that they were hired to help people, not to perform record-keeping functions.

On the other hand, the service agency regards paperwork and other organizational maintenance activities as central work responsibilities. Organizational maintenance activities "may or may not have anything to do with the adequacy of services to clients" (Brager and Holloway, 1978:13). However, such activities do offer politicians and the public a symbolic measure of effectiveness, whether or not actual accomplishment is evident (Rein, 1980). Symbols alone are often enough for the continuation of funding and thus the perpetuation, if not the expansion, of the service agency.

From the standpoint of the worker, however, the organizational imperatives operating in human service agencies contribute to a social welfare industry in the literal sense (Karger, 1981). That is, providers' skills and time become market commodities whose ultimate importance is identified through counts of units of service. Just as assembly line workers become alienated because of the objectification of their work, so too do service providers. Their malady has taken a new name: burnout.

Service providers not only experience cross-cutting pressures because of differing needs of clients and administrators; they also find themselves in cross-cutting, temporal frameworks (*see* Lewis and Weigert, 1981). That is, their use of time is perceived differently by clients and organizations. Service providers themselves may utilize yet a third temporal orientation; the policymakers whose decisions guide social welfare activities may operate on still a fourth timetable. What does this mean for service providers?

Not infrequently local, state, or national politicians have difficulty arriving at agreement over fiscal matters. Consequently, agency administrators may not know what types of services will be funded or what level of funds will be available until shortly before funding proposals are due. The federal legislative practice of continuing resolutions only prolongs this uncertainty. This situation creates a sense of time panic (Lyman and Scott, 1970) in an agency; all personnel may have to be mobilized to put a proposal together at the last minute. Employee mobilization for the tasks of proposal writing and statistical compilation interferes with the usual provider-client routine. It is likely either to disrupt services temporarily or create role strain and overload for those providers who simultaneously discharge their service functions. Also during this time some clients may experience emergency situations that require immediate attention from a service worker. In short, service workers are frequently caught in the temporal middle. In such cases the organizational timetable will take precedence over client needs, barring legitimate client emergencies. Still, the service provider is straddled with the difficulty of trying to resolve these conflicting demands. This accounts in part for their prevalent complaint of lack of time.

The preceding argument has focused on the need for temporal coordination due to simultaneous but conflicting time demands. Service providers also labor under sequential time demands that are at odds with one another. The uncoordinated nature of funding is an illustration of unsynchronized sequential time demands; it is one possible reason for providers' complaints about lack of resources to perform their jobs adequately. A single program may be operated through several funding sources whose funding cycles do not coincide. As a consequence, agency administrators may not know from one quarter to the next how much money will be available to operate specific programs and services. This uncertainty leads to fiscal conservatism by the administrator that may take the form of denial of additional funds to workers' programs. However, workers are likely to perceive such denial as lack of understanding or stinginess rather than good administration. For the service provider, fiscal conservatism merely translates into having to deny services to people.

At times the lack of funding for particular programs is also a reflection of the conflict between client and agency needs. One of the interviewees noted, for example, that her specific program always loses out to another program in the competition for funds. The latter program is already a successful and highly visible service, one from which the agency has developed a good reputation and of which the local community is proud. Its smooth operation does not require additional funds but it always seems to receive them anyway. The expansion of a program that fosters favorable community relations undergirds the agency's visibility and perceived success, even if such allocations are not consistent with the changing needs of clientele.

Mandates, Rules, and Regulations

Another area of service provider complaint is mandates, rules, and regulations. Complaints focus on the lack of discretion or autonomy in the provision of services to clients and the level of paperwork related to mandated reporting systems.

The possibility of conflict between organizational needs and client needs has already been noted. Because of this, it is not in the interest of agency supervisors or administrators to allow a great deal of discretion by the field worker. If such discretion were allowed, the provider might work in ways beneficial to clients but not necessarily supportive of the organization's needs. Workers might even use such latitude to challenge the agency's mode of operation or the rules that guide it. In the absence of strong worker alliances, administrators will predictably make decisions that reduce provider discretion and guarantee compliance with rules and regulations; to do otherwise could jeopardize agency funding or bring reprisal from policymakers.

There is another reason why it is unlikely that service providers within the current system of human services will get out from under the yoke of mandates, rules, and regulations. Providers are ultimately responsible to the public by virtue of their employment in a public agency (Howe, 1980). Thus, it can be argued that they are employed not to be altruistic and innovative, but rather to carry out the wishes of the populace as expressed in social policies. In effect, they are charged to be dirty workers.

The competing demands of paperwork and direct service provision have been discussed in an earlier section. Since paperwork is the medium through which service agencies are responsive to policymakers and funding sources, it will persist, if not increase. (In Chapter 4 political reasons are given for this claim as well.) It is sufficient here to note that when paperwork takes priority over the provision of services, the primacy of organizational needs over those of clients is once again demonstrated.

PROFESSIONAL AND ORGANIZATIONAL NORMS

Service workers theoretically could resolve the demands of competing groups by reference to appropriate normative or ideological systems. However, the norms of the profession of social work, or one's idea of those norms, and the norms of being an agency employee are just as likely to conflict as are client and agency needs. As will be seen, the inability to resolve competing normative systems is also a probable cause of certain worker dissatisfactions.

The behavioral expectations associated with being an employee of a publicly funded agency revolve around "obedience to the law as stated" (Rein and Rabinovitz, 1978:309) and as interpreted by one's supervisors. On the other hand, as noted in the preceding section, the 1979 Code of Ethics of the National Association of Social Workers maintains that the service provider's primary responsibility is to clients, a responsibility detailed at length in the code (*see also* Wilensky and Lebeaux, 1965). The brief section of the code that outlines social workers' responsibility to employers and employing organizations mentions only that one *should* work toward improvement of agency policy, procedures, efficiency, and effectiveness; *should not* work in or with an organization negatively sanctioned by NASW; *should* work to prevent or eliminate discrimination; and *should* use agency resources scrupulously. No explicit mention is made of how one should behave in situations of conflicting interests between client and agency, except for the general statement of client primacy.

In short, service workers experience contradictory messages from two primary normative systems related to their work: the norms of the profession versus the norms of the organization (e.g.,

Robin and Wagenfeld, 1977; Lubove, 1969). Their dilemma, similar to that which Schelling (1974:90) describes for businesses, "is not always between some selfish temptation and some obvious responsible course. The choice is often a policy decision" about which normative system will prevail under what particular circumstances. Rein and Rabinovitz (1978:315) note that these competing norms have been perceived as checks and balances so that one normative system would not dominate policymaking and service functions. They argue instead that "the general result is not a sense of protection against arbitrary behavior but primarily a widespread sense of frustration." Consequently, tensions between these two normative systems help to explain several of the dissatisfactions service workers describe.

Client Characteristics

As detailed earlier, two particular client-related characteristics that frustrate service providers are client dependencies and provider lack of control over relationships with clients.

One of the tenets of the NASW Code of Ethics is that social workers should facilitate self-determination insofar as possible by the client. Thus, when clients behave in ways that providers define as unnecessarily dependent, they represent an obstacle to fulfillment of the normative obligations of the profession. Ironically, many of the social policies that service agencies implement operate to enhance rather than diminish client dependency. From an organizational perspective the fulfillment of service providers' work can require the perpetuation, rather than the alleviation, of client dependencies on service workers and service agencies.

Workers' frustrations over the lack of control in provider-client relationships can be traced in part to the expansive norms of the social work profession, as well as workers' strong personal service orientations. Both of these factors contribute to the tendency of some service personnel to develop overcommitments (Marks, 1977) to their clients. That is, their responsiveness to clients' needs and demands becomes virtually open-ended. Further, insofar as clients are also heavily oriented to and rewarded by the provider-client role relationship, they will tend to expand their needs and demands indefinitely (Lipsky, 1980; Marks, 1977). As a consequence, the provider is likely to feel out of control of the service situation. (Chapter 4 argues that symbolic, ambitious social legislation operates to reinforce this situation.) As previously detailed, clients are not the only constituency the service agency employee has to please; their lack of control over this group will generate tensions in their attempt to respond to the organization. The felt lack of control is intimately related to the expressed frustration of lack of time, which will be discussed shortly.

Agency Problems

Just as competing client and organizational needs generate differing perspectives within an agency, so, too, do conflicting professional and bureaucratic norms. Organizational norms call for efficient execution within certain parameters of the social policies an agency implements. Administrators view acceptable worker behavior as the ability to perform service functions according to the guidelines of both the agency and its funding sources. From the vantage point of the worker, however, acceptable performance revolves around the ability to meet client needs. These needs are not necessarily consistent with, and sometimes conflict with, administrative perspectives regarding what the agency can do. The conflict is not so much, as some providers claim, that superiors do not really know what is going on at the direct service level; rather, the differing perspectives are more an issue of the primacy of differing normative systems for line staff versus administrators.

Lack of Resources

As remarked on in an earlier section, service providers are temporally caught in the middle between clients and employers. Each makes certain demands on the physically limited resource of provider time, and the service worker has to resolve these competing demands. Insofar as the provider holds strong commitment to both professional and organizational norms, adequate resolution of time demands will not readily occur because there will be no ideological justification for choosing one demand over another. Consequently, service workers will predictably experience a shortage of time for attending to the demands of both sets of role partners. The perceived shortage will seem even more acute if both sets of role partners generate ever-expanding demands. Earlier, the case was made for this likelihood on the part of clients. Growing demands are also likely on the part of agencies now that human services are confronted with the orientation of doing more with less that characterizes contemporary politics and budgetary concerns (*see* Chapter 6).

Mandates, Rules, and Regulations

Mandates, rules, and regulations are not necessarily troublesome. Rather, they become so for the service worker when they come into conflict with professional norms. For example, directives that establish firm program priorities, target recipients, resource levels, and other similar requirements undermine the service provider's ability to respond to individual clients according to their particular circumstances. As Bardach (1978:370) notes, "the more diverse the local settings and institutions being regulated, the harder it is to write reasonable rules and standards. Rules that are reasonable for one subclass of regulated organizations will be unreasonable for another."

So it is with mandates regarding targeted clientele. When client circumstances fall outside the boundaries of the directives, the provider is formally prevented from being responsive to the client. Yet, violation of directives in order to obtain goods or services for clients could possibly lead to reprimand by one's supervisor or loss of one's job altogether.

These sanctions are most likely to be employed if the possibility of detection exists; that is, if agency credibility is threatened. If it is not, then supervisors, who themselves may have been direct service personnel, can choose to overlook such discretionary behavior. Lipsky (1978) maintains that unauthorized discretion by direct service personnel is most likely to go unchallenged if (a) public policies emphasize decentralization, (b) the policy in question is not a high priority with supervisors, and (c) discretion is utilized during periods of policy shift.

SEMIPROFESSIONAL OCCUPATIONAL STATUS

From the perspective of political economy, service workers are viewed as "surplus population," just as their clients are (O'Connor, 1973). That is, many present social service personnel would find it difficult to obtain employment were it not for the elaborate social welfare apparatus of the government. There simply would not be an abundance of private sector jobs to absorb public service employees. Thus, providing government services accomplishes two purposes: it affords work to those who might otherwise be without it, thereby keeping them from being needy; at the same time it allows some level of assistance to others in need. In this way the provision of public assistance is said to be a self-correcting mechanism for a political economy that generates predictable unemployment.

The view of public service personnel as surplus population suggests that the occupational status of these workers is unlikely to be high. Another way in which service providers find themselves caught in the middle, then, has to do with their occupational status. Various aspects of their work can be viewed as professional in nature, while other work dimensions are decidedly similar to those of nonprofessional jobs. Service provision and social work have come to occupy a place in the classification of occupations known as the semiprofessions (Etzioni, 1969; Ritzer, 1972). Certain attributes that the semiprofessions have in common contribute to particular frustrations reported by line staff of various human services.

Agency Problems

Service provider complaints about lack of input into agency decision making and little discretionary latitude are complexly interwoven into the nature of the semiprofessions. Simpson and Simpson (1969) argue that the predominance of females as service providers enhances the likelihood of bureaucratic control over service work for the following sexist reasons: (1) the general public is less willing to grant discretionary latitude to women than to men; (2) females are seen as less intrinsically committed to the instrumental work role and therefore require more supervision; (3) females are less likely, because of career interruptions, to maintain updated knowledge about their work and therefore require more supervision; and (4) it is culturally normative that women should defer to men on the job, from their agency administrators, who are likely to be male, all the way to the policymakers, who almost certainly are male (*see* Edelwich, 1980).

The recruitment of more males into direct services might lead to greater autonomy for service workers. However, both Simpson and Simpson (1969) and Toren (1969) do not foresee the likelihood that men will enter the field in significant numbers. In the first place,

> the relation among the existing sex ratio . . . and the generally low prestige of social work is circular and cumulative: social workers are accorded less autonomy on the job, in part because the majority of them are women; on the other hand, because of more bureaucratic constraints and less prestige, the profession finds it difficult to recruit more men into its ranks. (Toren, 1969:157)

The issues of low pay and short job ladders for upward mobility for service providers also enter into this equation. In part because females predominate in social work, pay scales have been relatively low (Galper, 1975) and job ladders limited (*see* Kanter, 1977). So long as salaries remain inadequate and the chances for mobility low, the large-scale recruitment of males to direct service provision is unlikely.

Second, Simpson and Simpson (1969) note that the mystique of helping people involves attitudes and behaviors that have traditionally been associated with women's roles rather than men's. Service work is said to appeal "to the heart, not the mind" (Simpson and Simpson, 1969:203; *see also* Wilensky and Lebeaux, 1965). Insofar as this mystique about service functions is coupled with sex role stereotypes, another barrier exists for the recruitment of men into service work.

In short, part of the agency-related problems that service workers experience are a manifestation of occupational stratification and discrimination on the basis of sex. Service employees, both male and female, are affected at the agency level by the broader society's perceptions of, expectations about, and behaviors toward workers within particular occupational statuses.

Lack of Resources

The expressed lack of time noted by service providers is also related to certain attributes of semiprofessional occupational status. Simpson and Simpson (1969) characterize semiprofessionals as humanistically and holistically oriented to their work; that is, the service motive is prevalent. Serving others represents a major source· of job satisfaction. Insofar as this description is true, service providers are likely to take an expansive approach to their jobs. They will try to address whatever needs their clients have or they perceive their clients to have, even if doing so means having to stretch guidelines, put in extra hours during a workday, or go to undue effort. As noted earlier in this chapter, they will develop what Marks (1977) calls an overcommitment to the client-provider relationship. Clients who respond to this overcommitment by generating further demands or requests for services reinforce the service motive and expand the service function. Once these dynamics are set in motion, the service worker begins to experience a lack of time.

The problem of time for overcommitted service providers is similar to that experienced by high-status professionals such as medical doctors. Zerubavel (1979) describes high-status work as characterized by flexibly defined temporal boundaries, unclear separation between work and private time, diffuse responsibilities that are increasingly time-consuming, lack of protection of one's private time from intrusion by clients, salaried pay scales that allow for no overtime compensation, and lack of caretaker interchangeability so that other workers are not perceived as adequate substitutes in the performance of service functions. Zerubavel also notes, however, that high-ranking workers typically have various filtering devices, such as secretaries and receptionists, to protect their public time. While this is true for occupations such as medicine, the case is not so definitive for service workers. Ironically, the very ways in which service workers are more like professionals than not are the very ways in which similarities prove dysfunctional. Lower status jobs, with rigidly defined hours, overtime compensation, and interchangeability of role performers are better protected from the problem of lack of time and accompanying overcommitment to work roles than is the job of service provision.

In addition, the complaint of lack of funds can be understood to derive in part from semiprofessional status. Two characteristics of that status are relevant in this regard and are intimately intertwined. The first is the humanitarian motive assigned to the service semiprofessions, or the view of the social worker as giver (Kerson, 1978); the second is the prevalence of females in service work roles.

Although inadequate funding can be traced to cultural ambivalence about welfare work (*see* Chapter 4), it is also associated with the belief that service provision is a charitable enterprise motivated and supported by humanitarian concerns. As such, it is expected to rely on donations, volunteers, and good will as much as on government support. There is some question about the practicality of voluntaristic efforts today (Bergmann, 1981). There is also doubt about the extent of good will efforts and financial support forthcoming from highly profitable organizations (Broadway, 1981). Nevertheless, two assumptions underly a variety of social welfare policies. It is assumed that corporations, local communities, and religious groups will offer welfare assistance at requisite levels; therefore, it is also believed that government expenditures for human services should primarily be in the form of seed or safety net money. Insofar as these assumptions are mistaken, service providers will continue to experience inadequate funding as a work-related frustration.

Further, the fact that women predominate as line staff in service agencies contributes to the underfunding of services. Women's participation in the labor force has been misperceived as being generated by altruism, boredom, or the desire for supplementary spending money, rather than by necessity. The service role, then, came to be packaged in the symbols of volunteerism. If service providers can be thought of essentially as volunteers, then their humanitarian motives should enable them to do more with less, and to be paid less. There is evidence that some women may accept this stereotype. In a study of teachers in the state of New York (Fiske, 1982), men were twice as likely as women to cite low salaries as a major complaint about their work. One eventual outcome of the symbolic process of downgrading women's work is inadequate funding for service provision.

There is an ironic twist to this line of thought. Insofar as the sexist perceptions of the essentially female service force prevail, additional funds may be channelled into new or existing service programs rather than worker raises. In effect, by addressing worker frustrations over the lack of funding for services, the worker's strongest self-interest is undermined. How the service agency fares under such allocation strategies is problematic. On the one hand, its ability to undertake new initiatives or to further those already operating is likely to contribute to its credibility, visibility, and territoriality. On the other hand, stagnant worker salaries can generate worker dissatisfaction and employee turnover. When the labor market is constricted and service worker mobility is limited, the latter outcomes may be seen as acceptable trade-offs for the former accomplishments. Further, worker altruism may promote the preference for the channeling of new funds into services. The long-range result of such a choice, however, is the perpetuation of the semiprofessional status of service work and the attendant recruitment of those whose presence in that work force justifies professional marginality (i.e., those whose skills or occupational mobility are limited or whose motives are voluntaristic in nature).

In sum, being caught in the middle between certain structures, norms, and statuses generates predictable dilemmas and frustrations in the day-to-day experience of service work. The very arrangement of service work is problematic to the functions of service provision. This is not the full picture, however. The next chapter enlarges the perspective by examining contradictions built into the policies that service providers are expected to implement.

Chapter 4

THE ENVIRONMENT OF SERVICE WORK
Politics, Culture, and History

This chapter discusses how specific characteristics of social policies are the sources of several of the problems identified by service workers in Chapter 2. The policies in turn are reflective of larger political, cultural, and historical dynamics that impact on the social welfare enterprise in America. A basic premise of what follows is that events in the political and cultural areas of society have traceable implications for service workers. These implications include the inability of providers to carry out their responsibilities with a relative degree of ease and efficiency and the unlikelihood of client success in interaction with the service worker.

POLICY SOURCES OF WORKER DISSATISFACTIONS

Historically, social welfare legislation has taken on a variety of forms, addressed diverse target groups and social issues, and ebbed or thrived according to the particular economic and cultural climate of the day. Despite such variations, certain common themes characterize contemporary public welfare policies. Several of these themes, or characteristics, contribute to the difficulties of day-to-day service provision: (1) symbolic and ambitious goals, (2) universal entitlement, (3) intentional ambiguity, and (4) fragmentation. First each of these themes will be described. Next the theme will be shown to characterize particular welfare initiatives, including those implemented by the workers interviewed. Third, the specific impact these characteristics have on day-to-day service provision is described. Finally, how each statutory characteristic operates to the benefit of those who make the laws, and to other service system personnel, if not to the assistance of those who implement them at the level of interface with the client, is examined.

Symbolic and Ambitious Goals

Social welfare legislation is often characterized by stated intentions that are broad in scope, comprehensive in coverage, and ambitious in expectations. Such pieces of legislation can come to be known as "landmarks" or "benchmarks" of initiative in a particular area of reform. However, because such legislation is ambitious, it is frequently the case that resources provided for implementing it fall far short of what is required for its full enactment. While the stated ambitions remain symbols of the ideal, the limited funds allocated to operationalize the legislation undermine the likelihood of achievement of the originally stated goals (Sieber, 1981). A less sanguine description of such legislation notes that it

> project[s] images of adequate and reasonably comprehensive social welfare programming to taxpayers and . . . consumers, while in fact it limits support and assistance. (Lipsky, 1980:184)

Virtually any piece of legislation that represents a response to a newly identified social problem or to one that has taken on crisis proportions will be ambitious, and ultimately symbolic, in nature. For example, various authors (Holden, 1972; Arnoff, 1975; Cumming, 1976; Dunham, 1976) have described the mandate of the community mental health movement as "too broad and visionary and based on hope, reformist zeal, and political pressures" (Robin and Wagenfeld, 1977:24). Binstock and Levin (1976) cite the War on Poverty as another illustration of symbolic and ambitious initiatives. The Older Americans Act (OAA) under which the respondents are employed is yet another example of this theme. Indeed, Binstock (in *Future Directions*, 1980:32) argues that the comprehensive goals of the OAA have been coupled with a "funding distribution so thin as to have little impact on any given problem."

As seen in Chapter 2, service workers must mediate the consequences of high consumer expectations and inadequate resources for fulfilling those collective expectations. As a result, service providers have to deny consumers services. This function is not only distasteful and disheartening to social workers; it is also antithetical to the functions of their roles: it transforms them from altruists to dirty workers (Rainwater, 1967).

Ambitious but underfunded legislation not only creates frustrated workers, but also frustrated clients whose expectations cannot fully be met in the provider-client relationship. Immodest policies also produce worker competition within and between agencies over scarce resources for their particular programs. As already noted, many of the respondents expressed dissatisfaction with the level of funding for the programs they offer. However, instead of directing their frustrations to the policymakers whose limited allocations create their discontent, they tend to focus their ill feelings on the programs of fellow workers. Intraagency competition over funds can undermine the efforts of a single organization; interagency competition for funds can significantly reduce the possibilities for service coordination in the interests of clients.

In addition, the lack of resources contributes to tensions between line staff in an agency and agency administrators. While direct service providers tend to blame administrators for inadequate program funding (e.g., "They don't know the needs because they are not out in the field."), administrators generally believe that they are doing the best they can with the limited funds made available to them. In short, inadequate resources generate stress both horizontally and vertically within a service system.

While ambitious and symbolic legislation engenders problems for service workers, it is functional in at least two ways in the larger political arena (Binstock and Levin, 1976). First, its endorsement by politicians provides evidence to constituents that their representatives are interested in a particular social welfare issue. This becomes an increasingly important gesture around reelection time. Symbolic, ambitious legislation is likely to proliferate because of the growing number of interest groups competing for political rewards (Pressman and Wildavsky, 1979). Second, such legislation provides the general public and the targeted consumer group with symbolic reassurance (Edelman, 1977) that something is being done about an issue of concern to them. It placates them (Sieber, 1981).

In some cases, however, political progress is made simply by obtaining official recognition about the existence of a problem and an acknowledgement, if only symbolic, that action should be taken. As Rein and Rabinovitz (1978:324–325) point out,

> The very assumption that programs are designed to achieve measurable ends may in itself be unwarranted. . . . [A] program may fail in the short run while still influencing the trend of future developments.

At the very least, symbolic legislation guarantees that an issue is locked into the contemporary political agenda. Indeed, passage of any particular piece of legislation around sensitive or controversial issues may require that it be idealized and broad in character rather than concrete and definitive. Further, insofar as such policies are represented in exaggerated terms commensurate with their ambitiousness (e.g., a "landmark"), they are likely to neutralize potential opposition to them (Edelman, 1977).

Despite these larger political functions, however, symbolic and ambitious legislative goals create distinct problems for service providers who, along with consumers, bear the burdens of unfulfilled promises.

Universal Entitlement

Closely related to the elements of symbolism and ambitiousness is the policy characteristic of universal entitlement. Under universal entitlement, the target group of any particular piece of legislation is the broadest possible. For example, a national health insurance policy would cover all Americans, regardless of income, age group, or any other categorization. The American system of public education is perhaps the most visible universal social benefit program. From a more limited perspective, it is possible to talk about a program such as veterans' benefits as a universal entitlement program; that is, it is available to all veterans, regardless of income or age group. The respondents implement a universal entitlement program, the Older Americans Act. The OAA covers all aging Americans, regardless of social or economic status.

The attribute of universal entitlement, when coupled with inadequate funding for ambitious legislation, is another source of worker frustration. This frustration emerges due to lack of resources for such a broad base of potential clientele. Efforts to narrow the base are not always successful. For example, despite amendments to the OAA to target funds to the aging with the greatest social and economic need, "services cannot be 'means-tested' and access to these services is not uniformly restricted by specified eligibility criteria or intake procedures" (Armour et al., 1981:210). At the very least, targeting mandates are difficult to implement. One director of an Area Agency on Aging vented her frustration over this situation in the following way:

> Should we be concerned with the oldest, the sickest, the poorest, or all old people? ... I find myself in a dilemma. ... We have two sets of older people knocking at our door. One set are those who are the very vocal and able older people making their demands on the budgeting process. Then there are others who cannot get out and tell about their needs. Congress seems to respond to all older people, but what results [for both groups] are token programs. (Oriol, 1981:40)

The policy characteristic of universal entitlement is also related to workers' frustrations about certain client characteristics. It was noted in Chapter 2 that providers express dissatisfaction with clients they perceive as unwilling to help themselves and with clients who make unfair demands upon their time. Because all older people are entitled to benefits and services from the OAA, they may come to see these as rights, regardless of the objective level of need. The symbol of these services as rights is highly consistent with the rhetoric of the OAA legislation.

However, service workers operate with their own conceived hierarchy of entitlement. It is based roughly on level of need, as defined by the provider. Elders whom workers believe to be less needy than others are perceived as overdemanding. As such, they become sources of stress or frustration. Yet, it is often the less needy who readily take advantage of universal service programs (Estes, 1979).

For example, one study reports that two-thirds of all participants in national demonstration project nutrition sites funded through the OAA were active in their communities and had a variety of social contacts (Bechill and Wolgamot, 1972). This outcome occurred, despite the emphasis OAA implementers were supposed to put on reaching the socially isolated or nutritionally needy. A second study (Alfaro and Holmes, 1981) that utilized comparison groups provides even stronger confirmation of the claim that universal entitlement favors the less needy. Title XX of the Social Security Act is targeted for low-income recipients and provides funds for certain aging programs that are also funded through the OAA. However, some states have obtained group eligibility for the elderly; that is, Title XX funds can be used for the aging as a group, without the necessity of means testing. States obtaining group eligibility were found to have increased their services to elderly with higher incomes and to have become less likely than the non-group-eligible states to serve disabled clients, those living alone, and individuals below the poverty level. The authors conclude that the availability of free services on a group basis seems to encourage elderly with greater resources to apply for assistance. (*See* Nelson [1980] for further discussion of competition between the poor and nonpoor aged for Title XX resources.)

Insofar as universal entitlement is coupled with inadequate funds, workers are likely to experience demands on their time from emergencies. Once clients realize that competition for available services is keen, it is in their interest to employ the label of an emergency in order to secure the scarce resource they seek. From the client's perspective, the situation may in fact be seen as an emergency. However, from the perspective of the worker, who is familiar with a broad range of needs, the definition of emergency may have narrower parameters. So long as the definitions used by clients and workers differ, workers will experience certain clients as sources of dissatisfaction and frustration.

If universal entitlement creates strains for those who implement it, does it also have positive functions? Binstock and Levin (1976) note that the interests of politicians are served in at least two ways by targeting broad groups for welfare legislation. First, expansion of the target group may be necessary to garner sufficient support for passage of the legislation. Indeed, policy expansion, or dilution, is a classic means of overcoming power fragmentation among decision makers in order to pass a bill. Estes (1979) maintains that universal entitlement was necessary for getting the OAA passed because this enabled it to be distinguished from other welfare legislation of its time, particularly policies of the Office of Economic Opportunity. Second, politicians benefit from universal entitlement legislation in their ability to utilize it as evidence of their concern for a large number of constituents. Such evidence may be critical for the reelection of some politicians.

Universal entitlement serves certain interests of service providers and other agency personnel as well. A variety of studies document the preference of social workers for middle-class clients over low-income consumers (Rein, 1980; Chalfant and Kurtz, 1972; Willie, 1960). Further, Scott (1967a) notes the systematic bias of workers with the blind for clients who are either young children or employable adults. Insofar as universal eligibility allows for the priority selection of middle-class and high-potential constituents, some service workers may prefer it to means-tested programming.

The mix of clients that universal eligibility makes possible also provides the worker with diverse challenges and differentially demanding clients. In fact, the need for such a mix as a stress-reduction strategy is a recommendation pervasive in the literature on service worker burnout. Further, universal eligibility lessens the paperwork of service providers because it is unnecessary to perform detailed screening of potential beneficiaries.

Service organizations find favor with universal eligibility for at least three reasons. First, this policy characteristic reduces the paperwork required by elaborate client screening procedures, thereby lessening the overall administrative burden of the agency. Second, it becomes easier to coordinate different funding sources when there are fewer strings attached. For example, group eligibility under Title XX makes it considerably easier for agencies to align Title XX funds with those from the OAA. In fact, Alfaro and Holmes (1981) maintain that the aging network's push to obtain group eligibility was done to serve the needs of the agency rather than the needs of their elderly constituency. Third, universalism allows the agency to select from among a large pool of clients those who fulfill certain organizational needs (McKinlay, 1975). These are likely to be clients whose difficulties are the most malleable or who fit some predetermined demographic profile. Agencies are more likely to be perceived as effective when they have the opportunity to process the cream of the crop rather than when they serve clients whose difficulties are complex or entrenched (Scott, 1967a).

Finally, universal entitlement has certain advantages for the client population. A number of authors (e.g., Etzioni, 1976; Wolfensberger, 1972; Huttman, 1981) argue that universalism eliminates the stigma associated with service seeking because it does not require that one be labelled poor or needy in order to obtain assistance. The lack of eligibility criteria eliminates the possibility that someone will fail to qualify, despite having a circumstance of real need (Huttman, 1981). Universal services may be of better quality than those for the poor only, in large part because the nonpoor have power and influence to demand adequate provisions (Huttman, 1981; Titmuss, 1971).

In sum, while the policy characteristic of universal entitlement is a source of frustration for a number of service workers, there are trade-offs involved with it. In particular, universal eligibility addresses certain political needs of legislators, the work preferences of some service providers, specific administrative needs of service agencies, and selected concerns of clients.

Intentional Ambiguity

A third typical characteristic of social welfare legislation is intentional ambiguity, or the purposeful neglect of policy specification. This attribute is closely wedded to dramatic, symbolic policies that posit grand intent but offer little guidance for operationalization.

Ambiguity is troublesome for service personnel charged with implementing such legislation. As Rein and Rabinovitz (1978) note, the implementation process is typically complex and circular. These authors argue that

> In the absence of uniform, coherent objectives and overriding principles, an environment crowded with various legislative mandates may create a situation where the multiplicity of programs may cancel each other out. (Rein and Rabinovitz, 1978:328)

In their study of caseworkers for Aid to Families with Dependent Children (AFDC), Street et al. (1979) document the stresses caused by policy ambiguity. Suttles (1979:12) notes in the introduction to the study that

> Public welfare organizations often seem to be a mere aggregation of different rules and procedures that have been imposed by external pressure groups. This spectacular accumulation of rules and procedures makes life difficult and problematic for functionaries and recipients. What looks like goal displacement is frequently just a confusion of goals, strung together piecemeal by chronic reforms. . . . The net impact . . . is the cumulative growth of worker responsibilities and client hurdles. . . .

In a similar vein, Holden (1972) argues that the community mental health center mandate to help people with what are termed the "problems of living" is so broad as to be unrealistic, even if definable. Besides addressing this vague mandate, community mental health centers are expected to perform conventional psychiatric services; however, it is unclear which of these mandates should receive priority attention. Morris (1979) notes that Title XX of the Social Security Act, which funds personal social services, is ambiguous in at least two central respects. First, there is no clear guidance in terms of what specific services should be offered. Second, the act fails to indicate whether services should be delivered through a newly developed service network or through a preexisting service system. As a further example, the Elementary and Secondary Education Act, described by Bailey and Mosher (1968:99) as "a law unprecedented in scope," contains many uncertainties and contradictory criteria (Pressman and Wildavsky, 1979). Finally, the area of health services provides another illustration of legislation characterized by ambiguity. The National Health Planning Act of 1974, which set up local Health Systems Agencies, mandates them to make decisions that result in cost controls and that also improve the health of citizens in the community. It is not clear which of these priorities should be pursued most vigorously (Edington, 1980).

The ambiguity of the Older Americans Act, whose programs the interviewees implement, is manifested in several ways. First, it lacks clarity about who should be served, a dilemma emerging from the original act's universal entitlement and later amendments that prioritized subgroups of the aging for services (Armour et al., 1981; Estes, 1979). Second, ambiguity exists with regard to what efforts should receive greater emphasis, direct service provision or pooling and coordination activities (Armour et al., 1981; Estes, 1979; Hudson, 1974). Third, the OAA is unclear about the specific and unique functions of each level of its implementation apparatus (the Administration on Aging at the federal level, Regional Offices of Aging at the interstate level, State Units on Aging, Area Agencies on Aging, and local community service agencies) (Armour et al., 1981; Hudson, 1974; Fritz, 1979). Fourth, there is disagreement on how the accomplishments of the OAA should be measured, given the demand for national accountability on the one hand and a decentralized planning strategy on the other hand (Estes and Noble, 1978).

If the framers and interpreters of the OAA and similarly ambiguous legislation have not been clear with regard to critical issues, it is not surprising that workers at the local level experience confusion. This confusion surrounds what they or the programs they operate are supposed to accomplish, how it should be accomplished, and how they are to cooperate with other local service units. Such confusion eventually leads to stress, frustrations, and job dissatisfaction for a number of service workers. However, it is only "when we decide what it is that we are trying to accomplish" (Wilson, 1967:8), when objectives are clearly stated, that these kinds of bureaucratic problems will diminish.

Lack of job specificity and program structure are not the only problems resulting from legislative ambiguity. Demands for excessive paperwork grow out of this policy characteristic as well. When goals are ambiguous, accountability becomes problematic. According to Estes (1979:52), "The necessity to devise performance standards under conditions of intentional ambiguity . . . has led to sharply narrowing the focus of accountability. . . . " In effect accountability becomes reduced to a numbers count of units of service and assurances that certain regulations are abided by. Since goals are ambiguous, it is not clear what specific data might be needed for accountability; thus, numerous data must be amassed in case they are needed at some level of the elaborate administrative and oversight structure (Estes and Noble, 1978). This form of goal displacement, i.e., the emphasis on number of clients served and amount of funds expended, when coupled with the likelihood of numerous jurisdictions for whom such reports are required (Armour, Estes, and Noble, 1981), creates the large amounts of paperwork about which service providers complain. Yet, for all of the time workers spend in doing paperwork, the amassed data fail to produce conclusions about whether specific programming leads to desired results. Instead, the functions of monitoring and auditing come to replace evaluation as adequate oversight practices. The net result, from a critical perspective, is that "[t]he capacities of bureaucracies are overwhelmed and reduced to the caricature of filling out forms" (Suttles, 1979:9).

Thus, ambiguity in the original legislation, and in its multiple layers of interpretation across agencies and over time, creates distinct dysfunctions for workers at the level of direct services. However, the very discretion that social workers expect from their jobs (Lipsky, 1980) derives from certain types of policy ambiguities, particularly the call for comprehensive services. Because no agency can realistically provide comprehensive services, agency personnel are afforded wide discretion in the determination of programming priorities. Consequently, workers may have to settle for some trade-offs in order to obtain the discretion they believe will enhance their ability to accomplish local goals.

As previously noted, policy characteristics that are dysfunctional at the level of service provision are frequently functional for the politicians who devise the legislation. The same argument can be made for the attribute of ambiguity. First, the passage of intentionally ambiguous legislation is one way for Congress or other decision makers to "cope with an overload of popular demands for adopting policies of social intervention" (Binstock and Levin, 1976:519). Given continual demands from various interest groups for legislative attention, it becomes virtually impossible for policymakers to acquire detailed information about each specific issue to which they must respond. *Circuit breaker* legislation (Binstock and Levin, 1976:519), that is, an ambiguous policy that will be operationalized at various administrative and judicial levels, allows politicians to claim responsiveness to constituents and interest groups while at the same time passing on substantive decisions to others (Lowi, 1979).

Second, the endorsement of intentionally ambiguous legislation may be the politician's only supportive option if the issue is controversial and the legislator feels that some bill on an issue should be passed. Issues on which there are strong differences of political or professional opinion will only be passed if they are sufficiently diluted so that opposing powerful groups can reach compromise. In effect this strategy is "an effort to avoid conflict at the top by pushing it downward into the bowels of bureaucracy" (Suttles, 1979:14) or a means of diverting difficult decisions to occupationally protected decision makers such as Supreme Court justices (Dahl, 1958) and executive branch bureaucrats. However, it does enable the politician to claim responsiveness to relevant interest groups and to make a significant step in ensuring that the issue will remain on the larger political agenda.

Third, politicians benefit from the quantifications produced by paperwork. Numbers counts of persons served, programs operating, and funds spent are useful measures of achievement that enable politicians to symbolize the success of their legislative efforts. Statistics can evoke popular reassurance, even when they have little relevance to client experiences or programmatic outcomes (Edelman, 1977).

Although ambiguity creates certain problems for agency administrators, it can also operate to their benefit. Because agency goals are ambiguous, accountability is problematic. However, the preference for numbers counts and expenditure records by those with agency oversight lightens the administrative burden. As Levy (1970:172) observes,

> From the perspective of administration, all that is really required of [service workers] is that the statistical requirements are met, minimum tasks for clients are performed, and records are maintained so inspectors from the federal and state government will be satisfied that eligibility has been established, thereby legitimating reimbursement.

In short, administrators do not have to worry about an evaluation process that measures the degree to which a program or service has accomplished what it was intended to do. Rather, they need primarily to be concerned with the appropriate execution of internal organizational processes (Pressman and Wildavsky, 1979).

Further, in a climate of ambiguity it is possible for administrators to register organizational success by defining and operationalizing organizational objectives and interpreting quantified information in their own interests. According to Edelman (1977:80), "Evaluation of the achievement of vague objectives inevitably exaggerates results and the utility of services." Such maneuvering room with regard to accountability is functional for organization maintenance, whatever the actual level of the organization's performance.

In sum, while ambiguous legislation yields certain dysfunctions in the everyday routines of service providers, it also performs distinct functions for a variety of actors in the service system. Any attempt to clarify ambiguities, then, is bound to have trade-offs that must be considered against the functions that ambiguities serve.

Fragmentation

A final characteristic of social policies that generates worker discontents is *fragmentation*. Fragmentation can be defined as the proliferation of organizational units both horizontally and vertically to address the same or related issues. Fragmentation is likely to occur when there is an expansion of the implementation apparatus for a specific policy or when new organizational structures are created to implement newly legislated policies. Further, fragmentation exists in the social welfare enterprise because public agencies often have mandates similar to private agencies. The practical consequences of fragmentation are deleterious to social welfare efforts, as Pressman and Wildavsky (1979:110) note: "Given a large number of clearance points [for policy implementation] manned by diverse and interdependent participants, the probability of a program achieving its goals is low."

The problem of fragmentation in public services is not an ailment peculiar to contemporary American life. In 1863 the state of Massachusetts was concerned enough about its uncoordinated service organizations to create a Board of State Charities. The responsibility of this board included "investigating and supervising all of the state's charitable and correctional institutions and recommending changes that would bring about their more efficient and economical operation" (Trattner, 1979:76). By the end of the nineteenth century, sixteen other states had created bodies to overcome the fragmentation of their social welfare systems. Similar activity occurred in localities around that same time. Spurred on by the creation of a clearinghouse for relief-dispensing agencies in Buffalo, New York, in 1877, some 138 cities soon developed charity associations for the purpose of promoting cooperation and avoiding duplication of services (Trattner, 1979).

Nor is the problem of fragmentation peculiar to only a few service areas. For example, in the early 1900s, most states were described as having "an uncoordinated array of health districts and authorities," with New York alone having 500 to 600 separate public health boards throughout the state (Trattner, 1979:128). A management study conducted by the Department of Housing and Urban Development in 1969 found that the approval process for an urban renewal project consisted of about 4,000 steps in the bureaucratic maze (Rein and Rabinovitz, 1978:328). Current eligibility levels for clients across services or benefits are uncoordinated. Just because one person meets the criteria to receive food stamps or Medicaid, that same person may not be eligible for Aid to Families with Dependent Children (Huttman, 1981). Further, eligibility and benefit levels for programs such as Medicaid vary from state to state, making national accountability for such efforts problematic.

In uncoordinated service systems, fragmented services are characterized by (a) the dilution of funds across existing organizational jurisdictions, resulting in minimal programmatic impact and worker discouragement over the lack of funds; (b) confusion over which agency should perform what functions, resulting in the lack of specificity for program structure and for work roles within the agency; and (c) the ongoing attempt to coordinate activities with other units in the interest of coherent client services, contributing to the worker's perceived lack of time for direct service delivery.

Specifically, with regard to the aging service system in which the respondents work, Estes (1979:231-2) argues that fragmentation "results in an inability to treat any major problem coherently or holistically." Further, it does not provide organizations with "jurisdiction over areas that are vital to their assigned responsibilities." In fact, the Administration on Aging in the Department

of Health and Human Services experiences two major constraints
in addressing its mandate to coordinate national efforts related to
aging. First, it lacks statutory authority to make other agencies
comply with its recommendations, and second, it has limited discretionary funds for bargaining with other agencies in an effort to
consolidate resources or initiatives (Fritz, 1979).

There is a certain irony in the intentional creation of a parallel
aging service system that is set apart from other service networks.
The Older Americans Act calls upon its organizational units to
devote priority attention to the functions of pooling and coordination with other established agencies. In effect the OAA has created
a problem of fragmentation and charged its various administrative
units to overcome it at the same time that they address problems of
the aging. Ironically, the inability to achieve coordination is seen
as local organizational failure rather than as a design problem
inherent in the legislation and its implementation (Armour, Estes,
and Noble, 1981).

Efforts at coordination of services for the aging face major
obstacles because aging agencies have been established alongside
already existing community organizations that have occasionally
served older people. As a consequence, it is not unlikely that
organizational domains become even further entrenched, and competition over scarce resources becomes even keener when new
agencies are created to address formerly dispersed functions. New
agencies, regardless of their mandate for coordination, have to
expend significant energies on organizational maintenance and
political survival (Hudson, 1974). The latter task is made especially difficult by the relatively low political resources characteriz-
ing new organizations. In sum, overcoming fragmentation is a
difficult assignment for new agencies because considerable effort
must initially be spent on internal matters and the establishment
of credibility among organizations already in existence.

A fragmented service system is not without its functions, however.
First, the creation of new agencies around new policies provides
the opportunity for politicians to offer jobs to their supporters or
to sidestep entrenched bureaucrats who may give them trouble.
Second, a plethora of interest groups and middlemen benefit from
the proliferation of service organizations; new organizations offer

jobs or political legitimacy for the former and contracts and reimbursements for the latter. Third, the creation of new agencies to carry out new policies can avoid the organizational stasis of already existing structures and ensure the agency's commitment to new goals (Binstock and Levin, 1976).

THE POLITICAL AND CULTURAL BASES
OF SOCIAL WELFARE POLICIES[1]

The policy characteristics just described are the consequences of certain fundamental dynamics operating in American society. This helps to explain why the characteristics obtain across different kinds of social welfare legislation. The dynamics that underlie certain policy characteristics include (a) diversity as a fact of American life and (b) cultural ambivalence toward social welfare functions. The following sections explore how each of these background factors influences the development of social policies that ultimately prove troublesome for service workers and inadequate for intended beneficiaries.

Diversity as a Fact of American Life

The diversity of American life is a source of national pride; it has also contributed to fragmentation and related problems in social welfare. Diversity is reflected in a number of factors, including the system of state governments alongside the national government; the separation of church and state; the structure of Congress; the ethnic, racial, religious, and cultural diversity of the population; and the contention of interest groups for political favor.

The difficult birth of the United States occurred amidst heated debate about the role of individual states in relation to a federal government, or, alternatively, the role of a central government with respect to the several confederated states. In simplified form, it was a debate between the Federalists, who advocated centralized

---

[1]Specific historical references in this section come from Trattner (1979), unless otherwise noted.

power residing in a national government, and the so-called anti-Federalists, who believed that state power should be paramount and that the federal government should be subordinate in most matters to the states. The importance of this debate to the contemporary social welfare enterprise surrounds the issue of which of the levels of government should assume primary responsibility for charitable and humanitarian assistance. This debate has yet to be resolved.

In the early history of the United States whatever social welfare activities were undertaken by government typically occurred in localities, with occasional assistance from the states. This led to a diversity of programs, differing levels of assistance, and differing attitudes regarding social welfare and its recipients across local and state boundaries. As Trattner (1979:38) notes,

> Unlike Great Britain, Germany, and other European countries, the United States has had no single legal code affecting social welfare matters throughout the nation. Instead, it has had various state laws and court decisions which, on the one hand, have made for confusion, uncertainty, inefficiency, and tardiness in matters of social welfare, but on the other, have permitted flexibility.

By stressing states' rights and limited central government, the federal system, until recently, has minimized the role of the national government in assuming responsibility for aiding the needy. This is not to say that it assumed no responsibility, but that less was assumed in America than elsewhere. Since the states also supported relatively few measures designed to aid the unfortunate, towns, or other local units, and private citizens took on most of the welfare burden.

Typically, state governments came to assume responsibility when one or the other of the following situations occurred: (1) localities experienced large influxes of people, particularly immigrants, or (2) states felt that localities were providing inadequate or unequal assistance. Similarly, states began to look toward Washington for help as they began to realize that social problems were not constrained within state boundaries. The federal government itself was setting some precedent for its involvement with social welfare through limited aid to education and to victims of natural disasters.

Still, in 1854 after Congress passed legislation to provide assis-

tance for the mentally ill, President Franklin Pierce vetoed it, with
the explanation that the Constitution did not authorize the federal
government to undertake charitable initiatives. In 1931 President
Hoover upheld that position when encouraged to provide federal
unemployment relief at the outset of what was to become the
Great Depression. He based his argument against federal intervention not only on the premise of illegality, as did his predecessor,
but also on the concerns that such assistance would endanger the
financial status of the national government and would interfere
with the workings of natural economic forces. Within that decade,
of course, under new national leadership, the federal government
embarked on significant social welfare activities that set precedence for federal intervention for years to come.

In the 1960s the United States government further accelerated
its welfare activities because of its perception that provisions by
states were inconsistent and inadequate and, at times, discriminatory.
The 1980s are witnessing, with the advent of the Reagan administration, a significant challenge to the division of labor between the
states and the federal government with regard to social welfare
functions. The new federalism, which actually was initiated with
less drama and scope under President Nixon, embraces the belief
that national responsibility for social welfare should be significantly
limited and that states should assume the lead in most charitable
activities (*see* Chapter 6).

In sum, the debate over the location of responsibility for welfare,
which began with the formation of this country, has yet to be
resolved; rather, temporary arrangements come and go with the
emergence and decline of popular ideologies and political regimes.
As a result, service providers experience changing sources of
authority, shifting mandates, ambiguous divisions of labor, and
fragmented or duplicated service systems. President Reagan's proposals for a radical reorganization of welfare efforts have created
widespread confusion over who should do what. There is also a
general reluctance to undertake new initiatives during a time of
organizational transition, not to mention funding cutbacks.

Regardless of any changes forthcoming from the new federalism,
it is undeniable that this century has witnessed the growing legitimacy of the role of governments in human service provision.

Increasing expectations for governmental intervention pose certain drawbacks for service providers, clientele, and the larger public welfare system. In many ways public service organizations have co-opted informal primary support systems in terms of caregiving and service functions. The existence of formal service systems enables families to justify reducing their own commitments to needy members. The interchangeability of care givers (LaRossa and LaRossa, 1981: Zerubavel, 1979), or the array of those deemed responsible for individuals in need, has narrowed over time, with public agencies playing an ever-broadening role. This shift of responsibilities creates difficulties for human service personnel who are expected to perform affective as well as instrumental functions for their clientele. It also creates client expectations for personalized attention that is difficult to give, especially in light of heavy caseloads.

The historic separation of church and state adds further to the problems of social welfare in the United States. At the outset of this country, the church was perhaps the primary dispenser of charity and humanitarian assistance, a responsibility duly consistent with its institutional functions. Because of the religious diversity of this society, church efforts in social welfare are not likely to be coordinated. Indeed, social welfare efforts often are duplicated in the process of each church serving its particular congregation. Agencies proliferated in both the religious and secular spheres as state and national governments began assuming greater responsibility for social welfare. Within the same locale, it is not uncommon to see a duplication of efforts because of similar initiatives in both religious and secular domains.

In the 1800s an informal division of labor developed between the public sector and private agencies, which were largely of religious origin. At that time public assistance came to emphasize institutional care of needy populations, while private organizations provided home relief. Today an informal division of labor has emerged, roughly based on social class. Governments are more likely to provide assistance to the poor, and private charities are more likely to respond to middle-class populations. With the advent of federal funding opportunities for private organizations to provide welfare functions, however, the line between church and state has become less distinct. Nevertheless, the blurring of auspices has not mitigated the fact that public and private services frequently offer duplicated activities, thereby contributing to the fragmentation of the service system.

Within the federal government, the dispersed power structure of Congress contributes to service worker problems and welfare system inadequacies. It was noted earlier that power fragmentation is likely to produce social welfare policies that are intentionally ambiguous, serve largely symbolic functions, expand target groups, and proliferate service networks. Further, the specific deleterious consequences these policy attributes have on the daily lives of service providers and their clientele was noted.

Yet another source of social welfare difficulties derives from the ethnic, racial, religious, and cultural diversity of the American people (Wilensky and Lebeaux, 1965). Demographic and cultural differences have produced a plethora of private service agencies whose target populations are confined to particular groups. The importance of specialized agencies should not be underestimated: they play a significant role in the social integration of their populations, and they frequently address the needs of groups against whom other agencies have discriminated. Nevertheless, these organizations have often been put in place alongside existing agencies serving similar functions, thereby adding to the growing patchwork of human service organizations.

A final source of service system problems is the activity of hundreds of different interest groups seeking political attention and favors. The ideology of pluralism in American political life presumes that optimal social policies emerge from the freewheeling competition of interest groups vying for recognition and benefits. Despite this ideology, at least two negative functions of interest group behaviors must be noted. First, in order to respond to a growing number of interest group demands, politicians generate imprecise policies that must then be articulated within bureaucratic implementation structures (Binstock and Levin, 1976). These policies are symbolic and intentionally ambiguous; the difficulties they create for service providers and clientele have already been detailed. Lowi (1979) refers to the policy outcomes of interest-group liberalism as "nothing more than sentiments" (p. 56), "policy without law" (p. 92); yet these vague directives are the very ones that service providers ultimately must implement.

Second, the proliferation of interest groups, each of which is seeking its own ends, contributes to the fragmentation of the human service system. With different service groups, target populations, and specialized advocates seeking political favor, decision makers may placate the various groups by awarding them separate and specialized service structures. Whenever a new interest group emerges or a new need is identified, it can readily be addressed through the proliferation of new service networks. This political task is far less difficult than is the articulation of new needs, demands, and actors with existing, embedded service structures. What this politically expedient solution sets in motion, however, is the subsequent need for coordination by service personnel. Coordination is made all the more difficult by territorial rifts and intergroup and interagency competition spawned by the appearance of new service organizations.

In sum, various manifestations of diversity in American life provide the bases for service workers' routine, daily difficulties and dissatisfactions. Debates continue with regard to where primary responsibility for the provision of social welfare lies (federal versus state, public versus private) and how to respond adequately to the political demands of diverse populations and interest groups. In many ways public decision makers have generated the current problems of service personnel and the social welfare system by failing to resolve these debates and instead behaving in a politically expedient manner.

Cultural Ambivalence Toward Social Welfare

Throughout the history of the United States, ambivalence has characterized both public opinion about, and political postures toward, social welfare. Service work orientations have reflected ambivalence as well. Attitudes about social welfare have shifted pendularly over the course of this country's history and even more rapidly within the past three decades. A recent analysis of social work textbooks (Ephross and Reisch, 1982) reveals a spectrum of assumptions across books with regard to the sociopolitical nature of society, its relationship to the experiences of individuals and families, and the appropriate role of the service professions in undertaking social interventions. Ambivalence has provided the cultural framework from which social welfare policies arise.

A debate that has enlisted social workers, political reformers, and the public at large over the past two hundred years in the United States, and that has been the focus of attention in other nations for centuries, surrounds the causes of peoples' needs. At times the needy have been seen as responsible for their own plight and therefore rendered worthy of only minimal assistance. Alternatively, they have been viewed as victims of dislocation in a changing economic or social order and thus perceived as having a right to adequate public assistance.

These competing definitions reflect a fundamental schism of beliefs in the fabric of American cultural life. Huttman (1981) notes that there is a cluster of internally contradictory values to which many Americans subscribe. On the one hand there are such beliefs as the Protestant ethic, social Darwinism, laissez-faire, individualism, and America as the land of opportunity. Adherence to these beliefs readily leads to the conclusion that the needy are responsible for their own situation. On the other hand, quite opposing values and beliefs also dominate the United States' cultural heritage, including the beliefs in democracy and equality and a sense of collective responsibility. These beliefs underlie the perception of welfare as a right. These competing themes have been played out politically over the course of American history; they continue unresolved.

For example, early nineteenth century America embraced the perception of the needy as responsible for their own situation. This viewpoint was reinforced by the Protestant ethic that viewed poverty as a sign of indolence. As a consequence, the assistance offered the poor was minimal and stigmatizing. At this time there were also a number of proponents for the elimination of public assistance. It was their belief that public relief would destroy the incentive to work and would come to be seen as a right rather than as a charity. However, by the end of the nineteenth century, with the advent of heavy industrialization and urbanization and the development of the settlement house movement, attitudes had swung toward social and economic reform rather than charity and individual reform. Those in need were viewed as victimized by the conditions of their time. Consequently, community organization, public assistance, and government regulation of business were seen as vital to social reform and individual improvement.

With the professionalization of social work in the 1920s, the pendulum swung back the other way, and individual casework became the preferred service modality. Soon thereafter, because of the widespread distress of the Great Depression, social workers, politicians, and the general public came to realize that blame for impoverishment could no longer be placed at the feet of individuals, many of whom had been considered middle class. Rather, the orientation returned to viewing the needy as victims, and significant federal legislative efforts were undertaken to address the widespread dislocation of the day. With this legislation in place, social workers returned within a decade to a casework orientation, and the public and its politicians fell into the complacency of the 1950s. However, ideological shifts occurred in the 1960s when governmental assistance came to be seen as a right of citizens and a fundamental responsibility of the national government. Political thinking in the current decade, however, has once again swung toward an individualistic orientation, in part in response to fiscal concerns.

Just as there has been historical fluctuation regarding the causes of need and who should be helped, contemporary attitudes are inconsistent and, at times, internally contradictory. Recent opinion surveys show considerable attitudinal inconsistencies with regard to public welfare. For example, Ogren (1973), in a representative sample of adults in Los Angeles and San Francisco, found that (a) support for welfare programs was dependent upon whether or not the recipient was perceived as worthy, (b) respondents generally agreed that the poor were victims of circumstance at the same time that they thought the poor do not try hard enough, and (c) respondents affirmed a national obligation to an adequate standard of living for all citizens but favored welfare assistance primarily for those who could be rehabilitated.

In a similar vein, Cook's (1979) data from a stratified random sample of Chicago residents reveal the willingness of the public to support welfare programs, but under certain specified conditions. Those conditions seem to be evidence of true need, perceived deservedness of the recipient, lack of alternative means of obtaining assistance, and the likelihood that assistance will lead to independence. Data from a more limited study in Alabama (Klemmack and Roff, 1980) concur with these conclusions with regard to support for services to the aging. Finally, an analysis of public opinion data spanning two decades (Smith and Spinrad, 1981) reveals persistently held contradictory popular attitudes. On the one hand, a majority of Americans expresses support for almost every government social program, unless it is labelled welfare; while, on the other hand, they favor reduced government spending and lower taxes. Thus, current public opinion provides ambiguous direction for the enterprise of social welfare, just as history offers no definitive momentum. Rather, the conflicts and contradictions of two centuries are still being played out, if only in new wrapping.

Closely related to the debate about perceptions of the needy is the debate about what purpose governmental interventions should serve. The extremes of this debate correspond to the alternate perceptions of the needy just described and are labelled the social control and progressive perspectives of social welfare (Rochefort, 1981). During times when the needy are believed to be responsible for their own situation, the social control orientation operates. Levels of assistance are minimal, and programs are punitive and stigmatizing. The introduction of public workhouses in the 1800s, for example, were settings for the able-bodied poor

> where their behavior not only could be controlled but where, removed from society and its tempting vices, they would presumably acquire habits of industry and labor and thus prepare themselves for better lives. (Trattner, 1979:51)

The contemporary counterpart to the public workhouse is the work requirement states may impose upon recipients of public cash assistance such as Aid to Families with Dependent Children. Many of the mandated work settings represent dead-end work, and there is no monetary reimbursement for work performed (Storey, 1982; Wells, 1982).

It has been argued that government assistance, until recently, was a means of "regulating the poor" (Piven and Cloward, 1971). That is, relief was provided at various points in history in order to contain the potential for political upheaval that a large number of dislocated people represents. When that potential abated, relief programs subsided. This view suggests that the public function of helping people flows, not from humanitarian concerns, but rather from the political need for social control. In fact, Trattner (1979:94) argues that an important impetus of the child welfare movement of the 1800s and 1900s was "the fact that many citizens viewed the child as the key to social control." As a consequence of the social control orientation, assistance levels represent only what is marginally charitable without promoting degeneracy or what is politically feasible to discourage popular revolt. The welfare function of government in these instances is said to be residual, being called into action during those times that require efforts to insure social stability.

The progressive orientation to governmental assistance corresponds to the view of the needy as victims of economic or social circumstances. From this perspective, governmental welfare functions are seen as the institutionalized rights of the citizenry. As a consequence, programs flowing from this orientation are less stigmatizing than those derived from the view of welfare as a social control mechanism. Examples of initiatives representative of this philosophy are Social Security, veterans' benefits, and unemployment compensation. Piven and Cloward (1982) argue that the institutionalization of benefits such as these and their accompanying ideology of entitlement make them difficult, if not impossible, to eliminate or cut back, even with present concerns about the national economy.

In short, just as there are contradictory perceptions of the needy, there are also contradictory notions about government's appropriate posture toward those in need. The contemporary patchwork of social legislation speaks vividly to the irresolution of these perspectives. Quite aptly, Wilensky (1955) characterizes the United States as a reluctant welfare state, one whose cultural and historical traditions reflect considerable ambivalence toward the function of social welfare.

The contradictions just described have direct influence on current social welfare legislation. Politicians respond to popular ambivalence by devising vague initiatives with rhetorical appeal but without programmatic substance. In short, they pass intentionally ambiguous and largely symbolic welfare policies. Such legislation requires that specific programmatic decisions about these policies be hammered out within the bureaucracies of the implementation apparatus. This procedure allows lawmakers to "farm out most of their own hard decisions" (Suttles, 1979:10) and not have to resolve the debates themselves. Further, they do not have to choose ideological sides, which would serve to alienate one or another of their voting constituencies. Such a legislative stance is indeed politically expedient, a point that should not be minimized. It also reflects legislators' lack of understanding of the causes and effects of social problems and the means and ends relationships of programmatic options (Rein and Rabinovitz, 1978). Thus, legislators allow programmatic decisions to devolve to administrators whom they believe to be more knowledgeable. In either case, the outcome is legislation that is symbolic and/or ambiguous and that ultimately plays havoc with the daily lives of service providers and welfare recipients. Further, over the long-run, legislative responses to cultural ambivalence produce a pendulum effect, or a "shifting [of] action in a direction that entails renunciation of the [preceding] intervention altogether, including its basic values" (Sieber, 1981:64). The more rapidly the pendulum swings, the more confusion that is created in the social welfare enterprise.

Chapters 3 and 4 have looked at several areas of the social welfare system in order to understand how organizational, political, cultural, and historical factors contribute to service workers' frustrations and dilemmas. Having provided this broader context, the next chapter will return to the area of service provision and examine how the interviewees manage the stresses they encounter in their work. The coping strategies they employ, while interesting in their own right, become far more meaningful in light of the arguments developed in Chapters 3 and 4.

Chapter 5

THE MANAGEMENT OF WORK STRESS
Turning Public Issues Into Personal Troubles

The preceding chapters have developed the argument that many of the stresses experienced by public service workers can be traced to systems beyond interpersonal, day-to-day activity. In the words of C. Wright Mills (1959), those stresses are public issues rather than workers' personal troubles. This is a significant point both conceptually and practically. Conceptually, this distinction demonstrates how larger systems intersect with personal biographies and interpersonal activities to produce the social welfare enterprise; practically, this distinction poses very different kinds of remedial strategies for alleviating work stress than have heretofore appeared in the literature.

This chapter refocuses on the everyday world of service workers in order to look at how they manage the stresses inherent in their work. The coping strategies they use to get through the work day fail to address the influence of larger cultural and political systems on their work. Further, their use of individualized coping mechanisms serves to reframe public issues as personal troubles and place blame for social welfare inadequacies on the very people attempting to resolve them. This personalized conceptualization of work-related stresses has significant consequences for the operation of the service system and for the conduct of the larger social welfare enterprise. These consequences are explored at the end of the chapter.

Before looking at the coping strategies used by the respondents, it is instructive to see what suggestions are provided in the current literature on human services for the management of stressful work conditions. These suggestions are primarily contained in the studies of professional burnout.

STRESS MANAGEMENT AND BURNOUT

The remedies that researchers propose for burned-out service professionals have been confined largely to intrapersonal, interpersonal, and managerial efforts to alleviate stress. Such remedies are consistent with the causes of burnout that researchers identify, as noted in Chapter 2. These researchers have, intentionally or unintentionally, conceptualized the burnout experience as a personal trouble located in the microsystems of service work. While it cannot be denied that microsystems can present problems for service workers, it is not believed, at best, that a full picture of service worker conflicts can be drawn from focusing only on microsystems. At worst, the failure to look for larger issues as stressors results in an unintended stance in the professional literature of blaming the victim (Ryan, 1971), that is, blaming service workers themselves for being "battered helpers" (Lewis, 1980). What are the various recommendations made by writers on burnout to alleviate or prevent service work stresses?

The burnout literature suggests that there are a variety of intrapersonal strategies that individual service workers can initiate to improve their work situation and to prevent work exhaustion. One such approach involves preparing oneself for work stresses by maintaining proper physical and mental health. Obtaining regular exercise and proper nutrition are means for achieving or maintaining physical health; a major way to insure proper mental health is to strike a balance between work and social life (Bryan, 1981; Maslach, 1979; Freudenberger, 1974; Larson et al., 1978). Another such approach regards taking a realistic stance toward one's work. For instance, service providers are cautioned to set limits on the demands of others, reject the notion of being all things to all people, analyze personal feelings related to work, not set goals too high, have fun on the job, be spiritual about the work, engage in personal planning, and employ personalized stress management techniques such as meditation (Bryan, 1981; Edelwich, 1980; Maslach, 1979; Maslach and Jackson, 1978; Maslach and Pines, 1977; Larson et al., 1978). Still other intrapersonal responses to stresses of direct service work include seeking promotion to a supervisory position or terminating one's job altogether (Edelwich, 1980; Wasserman, 1971).

At the interpersonal level, two strategies have been offered for the alleviation or prevention of burnout. The first, which is pervasive in the literature, is the suggestion to develop support groups with coworkers in order to share concerns with, and to seek advice from, colleagues (Bryan, 1981; Cherniss, 1980b; Wasserman, 1971; Maslach, 1976, 1979; Maslach and Pines, 1977). A second strategy at the interpersonal level relates specifically to problems with clients. According to Maslach (1978), efforts should be made by the worker to promote client self-reliance rather than dependence on the provider and to insure from the outset of the provider-client relationship that there are explicit expectations regarding its nature and goals.

The burnout literature also offers a rather comprehensive list of strategies that can be employed in work organizations to prevent or alleviate the experience of burnout by service workers. These strategies relate either to the content of the work, to working conditions, or to work benefits. Regarding the content of work, it has been recommended that managers provide variation in the amount and nature of client contact, including shared responsibility for the most difficult client situations, and the rotation of direct contact and administrative duties (Cherniss, 1978, 1980b; Maslach, 1976, 1979; Pines and Maslach, 1978; Maslach and Pines, 1977; Larson et al., 1978). Working conditions could be altered to allow for shorter work shifts, time-out from work, a reduction in case load, increased use of volunteers, regular staff meetings for discussion of problems, group participation in agency decision making, the provision of feedback from supervisory and managerial personnel, and the use of realistic work descriptions in the recruitment of staff (Cherniss, 1978, 1980b; Maslach, 1976; Freudenberger, 1974; Pines and Maslach, 1978; Edelwich, 1980; Bryan, 1981; French and Caplan, 1972; "Career Burnout," 1980). Finally, suggestions for the improvement of work benefits include more pay, staff retreats, opportunity for career advancement, and ongoing training and development activities, especially in interpersonal skills and stress management (Maslach, 1976, 1979; Pines and Maslach, 1978; Larson et al., 1978; Maslach and Pines, 1977; Edelwich, 1980; Cherniss, 1980b; "Career Burnout," 1980).

This overview of recommendations is useful in two ways. First, these strategies can be compared with those actually used by service workers. Second, the impact the various coping mechanisms have on the execution of work responsibilities at the microlevel and on the conduct of the social welfare enterprise at the macrolevel can be explored.

THE ROUTINE MANAGEMENT OF WORK STRESS

The interviews with service providers in the field of aging revealed the use of diverse and elaborate means, both cognitive and behavioral, for the reduction and management of work stresses. The predominant coping mechanisms used by the respondents are role manipulation, role bargaining, norm violation, quasi theories, and comparisons. A less widely used strategy is taking a religious orientation toward one's work. Finally, a few individuals advocate for legislative change as a means of alleviating work problems.

Role Manipulation

Role manipulation refers to an individual's ability to determine when to enter or leave role relationships (Goode, 1960; *see also* Sarbin and Allen, 1968). The interviewees utilized several strategies of role manipulation to manage the stresses that work created. A primary way that workers sought relief from occupational stress was through *compartmentalization* of their work and nonwork roles and activities. A few service providers mentioned with pride that they allowed or encouraged colleagues or clients to call on them after regular work hours. However, numerous respondents talked about their need to get away from it all and to engage in very different pursuits after work hours, or to have some private time (Zerubavel, 1979a). Nonwork pursuits generally served the function of reenergizing them to return to work or enabling them to ignore or relieve the tensions of work that they had just experienced. Such strategies are comparable to burnout researchers' suggestions to separate one's work and personal life. Here is how several of the interviewees expressed this approach to coping with work dissatisfactions:

> I go home and... try to go out to a movie or watch a TV show or just get
> my mind completely off [work]. I do try to draw a line and say, "That's it;
> I'll worry about it tomorrow."... If I took it home with me, ... then [I'd
> take] out my frustrations on the family, and I try my best not to do that.

> [I] just [go] home and [amuse] myself with something else.... I enjoy
> working around the house, working in the yard, and things of that sort. I
> get a great deal of therapy getting out, giving care to the lawn, and busying
> myself with what I am doing. I also like music a great deal, and I lose
> myself in my music.

Another approach to role manipulation employed by service
workers in aging is the *elimination or abridging of role relationships.*
That is, workers seek, either temporarily or permanently, to cur-
tail work-related role relationships. Temporary curtailment occurs in the form of what burnout researchers refer to as time-outs,
such as the following quotations describe:

> When I reach a point that I feel my work is becoming too taxing, I
> usually take a day off, and that does it. I say to my supervisor [that]
> I need an annual leave day. And I'll take a day and I'll buy myself
> something or whatever, and when I come back I'm bursting with energy,
> and I'm ready to go. I'll usually do that maybe twice a month, just
> take an unnecessary day, just to goof off.

> [When I got to feeling burned out, I] took a vacation, just took a couple of
> days and went up to the mountains and camped, had a great time, and
> came back rejuvenated and ready to go.

With regard to time-outs, however, Lewis and Weigert (1971:446)
argue that they will be self-defeating if they are planned rather
than spontaneous. This is so because planning itself is often responsible for the sense of a lack of time.

The permanent form of curtailment of stressful work-related
role relationships, of course, is resignation from one's work. Several of the interviewees had, in fact, employed this strategy to
remove the stress of their previous service positions. Indeed,
documentation of high turnover rates for service workers is prevalent throughout the literature on burnout.

Another strategy that can be employed to manipulate one's role
obligations is *delegation* of certain obligations to others. Given
what is perceived to be a severe shortage of staff across agencies,
however, this approach is a luxury only few workers experienced.
As one worker in a newly formed service program expressed it, "I

would like to be able to accomplish a lot more. . . . What I'm trying to do recently is make myself delegate more responsibility to coworkers, and that takes some of the burden off me." A related posture is the refusal to seek more work responsibility than one currently has. One of the respondents, when asked about a particular service policy, replied, "The policymaking I leave to the policymakers." In that statement is the implication that she would not employ whatever discretion exists in her service role to capture further role responsibilities.

A final strategy of role manipulation engaged in by a few service workers is *extension*, or the expansion of some role relationships in order not to have to fulfill obligations of other roles. For example, a provider can claim the demands of paperwork in order to avoid attending a little-valued workshop or seeing a particularly troublesome client or coworker. Or, a worker may use demands outside of work to account for failing to put in as much time at the job as she once did:

> Well, now I'm reaching a time where my mother is living with me, . . . and I am reaching a point of wanting to learn how to schedule work as a job as other people see it so I have time for all my other responsibilities and even for my own just pure relaxation and fun. . . . [B]efore, when I didn't have other responsibilities, if I was not finished at six or seven or eight, there was no problem for me. I just stayed on until I was ready to go home, that kind of thing. But now I need to meet, say, like a six o'clock deadline, which is in line with what most people do when they are at work.

The commonality among all of these forms of role manipulation is that they enable the worker to activate or deactivate role responsibilities when they become too stressful. These behaviors are not unique to workers in aging; they have been reported in such diverse service professions as police work (Maslach and Jackson, 1979), teaching (Fiske, 1982), mental health (Pines and Maslach, 1978), welfare investigation (Levy, 1970; Pines and Maslach, 1978), health care (Zerubavel, 1979; Maslach, 1979), psychiatric nursing, poverty law, prison work (Pines and Maslach, 1978), child care (Pines and Maslach, 1978; Maslach and Pines, 1977), legal services (Maslach and Jackson, 1978), and psychiatric therapy (Larson et al., 1978), as well as among general social workers (Brager and Holloway, 1978; Wasserman, 1971).

Role Bargaining

While role manipulation refers to the activation or deactivation of selected roles, the strategy of role bargaining refers to the negotiation of performance level within a given role (Goode, 1960). Another way in which service providers manage the stresses of their occupation is to strike bargains with themselves or with others about the price of the work role, or how much can be expected of them in the performance of their work responsibilities (*see* Lipsky, 1980). The primary manifestation of role bargaining that emerged in the interviews is the limiting of workers' expectations regarding how much they can realistically accomplish on the job. In their own words

> I just tried to get through one day at a time. That was the only way I could accomplish anything because when you start to think, "What am I going to do Monday?" then it almost became more than I could do to get through Friday and Saturday and Sunday. . . . I would just take the priorities and let the other things pile up and just try to get through the things that needed to be done. . . .

> You begin [to cope] by saying to yourself [that] you're only one person. There is only so much that one person can do, so you just have to calm down and take it one day at a time and do what can be done.

> I think I've pretty much made up my mind that . . . the only way I can personally deal with [dissatisfactions] is to . . . just realize that I am only one person, and there are many, many more needs than I will ever be able to take care of. So I just deal with those that just seem to me to be the most important and vital at the time and just be glad that I am able to have some little impact.

The role bargains that these service workers strike with themselves represent a very different orientation to the work role than that with which one usually enters service work. Entering social workers, in contrast, may be bursting with idealism and expectations of having significant impact through human services; they may be willing to expend long hours beyond the regular workday in work-related activities; they anticipate the future with high hopes for positive and profound outcomes from their work. Once in the service system and confronted with routine dissatisfactions and disappointments, however, it may be realistic to limit one's expectations of what is possible in an imperfect service system. Indeed, some writers (e.g., Cherniss et al., in press) argue that potential service workers should be trained in advance with a more realistic picture of the work setting that they will enter.

Noticeable in the preceding quotations is the prioritizing of the various demands of the work role, or the bargaining that some responsibilities have a higher role price than others. Thus, another means by which service providers reduce stress is through negotiating which role responsibilities are more valuable to attend to than others and treating them accordingly (*see also* Zerubavel, 1976).

A further means of role bargaining to reduce service work stresses is maintaining a stance of detached concern. While none of the interviews reveal the use of this strategy, Pines and Maslach (1978) found it to be employed by a number of service workers. Detached concern refers to a level of role enactment (*see* Sarbin and Allen, 1968) that does not require complete involvement of the individual's psyche; neither does it require a cold, objective approach to the client. Rather, the service worker maintains empathy at the same time that s/he keeps professional distance in the client-provider relationship. This stance is what Halmos (1970:121) calls "noninvolved involvement," and is believed to be an appropriate way of preventing the service worker from being consumed by any given client. Detached concern has been noted in the work of mental health personnel, welfare workers, psychiatric nurses, poverty lawyers, prison personnel, and child care workers (Pines and Maslach, 1978).

Even greater detachment is noted by Levy (1970) in his study of welfare investigators. Their strategies of role bargaining include ritualistic decision making, or going strictly by the rules, and making home visits as brief and structured as possible. Street et al., (1979) and Handler and Hollingsworth (1971) also found a general pattern of ritualized treatment of clients by AFDC caseworkers, despite the substantial amount of discretionary authority associated with their work. Levy (1970:173) reports yet another form of role bargaining, which he calls "goofing off." Goofing off includes "frequent trips to the washroom, visiting workers on other floors, trips to the restaurant across the street for a snack, and continuous conversations with those in [the] immediate units" as means of passing the time on the job.

These latter forms of role bargaining represent "true role distance behavior" (Stebbins, 1975). That is, they are direct reflections of workers' negative attitudes toward the job or the client rather than calculated attempts, as in the case of detached concern, to estimate the appropriate role relationship between worker and client (*see* Munson and Balgopal, 1978). They are also behaviors typically displayed by workers in relatively powerless positions with minimal opportunity for upward mobility (Kanter, 1977).

In sum, the process of role bargaining enables service workers to negotiate, within certain parameters, the manner in which they will carry out their work. It is a means for reducing the stresses of service work insofar as it allows them to limit what they and others should expect regarding the level of their work performance.

Norm Violation

Another strategy workers use in order to reduce stress is norm violation. That is, workers knowingly behave in ways that are not in line with expected conduct or formal work requirements. A typical manifestation of this strategy is, in the words of one interviewee, "trying to do as much as you can . . . outside the guidelines." While it is acknowledged that funding guidelines are to be respected, going around or outside of the guidelines is a frequent occurrence (*see also* Brager and Holloway, 1978). It has been reported that welfare workers use procedures in every way possible to benefit the client, even to the point of falsifying records in the client's behalf (Levy, 1970).

As certain sociologists (Scott and Lyman, 1968; Stokes and Hewitt, 1976) point out, individuals who behave in deviant ways feel the need to account for their actions verbally by reinterpreting them in culturally approved terms. Verbal accounts fall into two basic categories: *justifications* and *excuses*. Justifications are statements that accept responsibility for the behavior but that make a case for its appropriateness. Excuses, on the other hand, acknowledge the possible inappropriateness of a behavior but claim that the perpetrator is ultimately not responsible for its occurrence.

Service providers who reported stretching or violating guidelines used the justification of a *claim of benefit* to explain their behavior. That is, while they recognize that their actions fall outside strict work rules, they justify violating the rules in the interest of helping clients:

> There are some times we may do things outside of the order. You know, Miss Jones needs to have some things done for her or with her, [so I try] to meet her needs [by looking for] some leeway.

> The program that I was working for was funded by [one source], . . . and there were certain areas of the city that we were supposed to work in and certain areas we were not. . . . There were several times that we wanted to help somebody in a certain area of the city and weren't supposed to because they didn't live in the right neighborhood. . . . [But] we adjusted to it somehow by saying we were doing [a community project] for people in the neighborhoods we were supposed to be helping [when people in other neighborhoods could benefit as well].

Another form of norm violation is the development of negative feelings by providers toward clients in order to reduce the stress of the demands made upon them. Burnout researchers have identified such negative feelings as both a means of coping with stress, as well as an outcome of it. Interviewees who admitted such feelings justified them through a *denial of injury*. That is, while acknowledging that negative feelings toward clients are not appropriate in their work, the providers rationalized them as being harmless. Responding to the interviewer's question of whether the worker ever had negative feelings toward clients, one worker answered: "Yes, I think so. It stems primarily from impatience. I try to control it. I don't believe I'm guilty of letting it affect my ability to serve." Several others mentioned that they would quit their jobs if such feelings threatened to erode their work performance. Typical of this attitude is the following comment:

> If I get to a place where I'm going to be screaming at [clients] or saying something that will hurt their feelings, I'll quit first. I won't do that. But as long as I can maintain it, and the burnout is just within me, if I can keep it in me and not show it to them, [then I will stay].

Perhaps the most serious form of norm violation exhibited by service workers is physical abuse of clients. There is nothing in the interviews to indicate that such behaviors are engaged in by these workers, but such activity frequently makes the headlines of the popular media when it becomes highly visible or flagrant. In such instances it is common to hear the perpetrators of abuse account for the behavior through either a claim of benefit (e.g., bringing someone back in line or to their senses, doing it for their own good) or a denial of injury (e.g., it didn't really hurt them). In fact, Edelman (1977) argues that such verbal accounts are a central element in "the political language of the helping professions." By use of neutralizing language, service providers can exert power and control over their clients. Edelman focuses particularly on personnel employed in prisons, other correctional settings, mental facilities, and medical settings to argue this contention.

Still another type of norm violation that serves as a stress reducer is low-level performance of one's work. This strategy is also a form of role bargaining. Low-level work performance is reported throughout the burnout literature as both a stress reducer and an outcome of having burned out. The most likely way that service providers account for low-level performance is through the use of excuses, especially *appeals to biology*. As noted in Chapter 2, the complaint about lack of energy to complete work responsibilities can be an excuse for inadequate work performance, as can the claim of being burned out. Lack of time is an excuse for a poor work performance that appeals to laws of physical nature. Whether service providers' excuses are legitimate is problematic, they may instead be alibis masking low commitment to work responsibilities (Marks, 1977; 1981).

Quasi Theories

Quasi theories are verbal conceptualizations that attempt to create order in a disorderly situation (Hewitt and Hall, 1973). When service workers perceive their work as confusing, disorderly, or troubling, they may turn to quasi theories in order to reduce tension. Quasi theories take the form of ad hoc explanations for troublesome situations; they are used to make sense of these situations and to provide some hope for their improvement. In particular, the respondents employed the quasi theories of communication and of time to make some sense of their work difficulties, and thereby to ease some of its attendant stresses.

The *quasi theory of communication* involves the belief that work dissatisfactions will be alleviated through improved communication among coworkers and between service providers and their superiors. The former strategy is heavily recommended throughout the burnout literature where it is referred to as the development of support groups in the work setting. Merton (1957) refers to it in role theory as "mutual support among status-occupants." The belief is that work stresses can be reduced simply by talking to coworkers about troubling situations. From a somewhat different angle, some workers relieve stress, or believe that it will be relieved, by talking with their supervisors or administrators. These strategies are exemplified in these comments:

> Well, I've always been good at telling people how I felt, so I just talked to people about [work frustrations]. . . . [J]ust by telling people and sharing it with other people [helped relieve stress].

> [I handle dissatisfactions by talking] with coworkers, and I talk with managers and directors of other sites, and I talk with my coordinator, and I go home and talk with my husband. Out of all these people, sometimes I come up with some good answers, some solutions.

> I think it's probably not uncommon for all of us to sit around once in a while and just bitch about the problems that we are having and feel good that we did that for an hour or so. Then we all go our merry way back into our work. I guess it helps sometimes to know that we are all in it together.

One of the reasons that conferences with supervisors or conversations with coworkers can be fruitful stress reducers is that service providers can pick up advice about ways to account for their own nonnormative conduct. In addition, talk with coworkers enables service providers to understand that others experience the same predicaments and dissatisfactions, thereby rendering one's own discontents less severe. The supportiveness derived from talking with others has been reported with a variety of service personnel: health care staff (Maslach, 1979), legal services workers, poverty lawyers (Maslach and Jackson, 1978; Pines and Maslach, 1978), child care workers (Pines and Maslach, 1978; Maslach and Pines, 1977), welfare workers, psychiatric nurses (Pines and Maslach, 1978), and general social workers (Wasserman, 1971).

The *quasi theory of time* articulates the belief that "time itself creates and dissolves problems" (Hewitt and Hall, 1973:371). If one is patient, a problem should go away. This quasi theory is employed by a number of the interviewees as a means for handling the stresses that confront them on the job:

> I'll sit down and try to work out my own solution [to a problem], . . . but a lot of times when problems come up, you find that you don't have to think about that problem. It solves itself in the course of a day or in the course of a week. . . . [S]omething just comes up, so why, then, you stop and think, why should I worry about it?

> I don't worry about the day-to-day process because I know that if [work] doesn't get done today, it will be done tomorrow. If it doesn't get done tomorrow, it'll get done the next day. So it will be done.

In sum, quasi theories stabilize the work situation and minimize its attendant stresses and conflicts by providing service workers with ways of explaining discrepancies between work ideals and actualities.

Comparisons

Yet another way in which service workers manage their daily conflicts is through the use of comparisons. Comparisons take two forms: either service providers compare themselves or their work to other individuals or work settings, or they compare their current situation to their situational alternatives (Thibaut and Kelley, 1959). When comparison is favorable, workers appear less troubled by the inherent conflicts of their work.

A few of the respondents expressed some degree of satisfaction with their work because they compared themselves favorably to others. For example:

> When I compare myself with my colleagues and former classmates, I feel I'm achieving as much as they are. At one point in my life, I didn't think I was. . . . And when I compared myself [then] with other people in my age bracket, they seemed to be doing so much more, more gratifying kinds of things. But now I feel right in tune, right in step.

Several other interviewees neutralized work stresses through comparison of the programs in which they work with social service programs in general:

I guess that there are problems in any social service program.... In any job there [are] going to be some [frustrations and problems]. You are not going to have everything like you want it, when you want it.... If I went into something else, who's to say that that would be any different from what I've already been doing?

[N]o matter where you work, no matter what kind of agency you work for, the need is always greater than you are able to provide, and you are in the position to decide who gets services and who doesn't, setting up priorities, trying to do the best job you can do with whatever limitations you are working under.... I don't really think that you can get away from that sort of thing.

The other form of comparison that reduces discontent is comparison of one's current situation to alternative work or unemployment experiences one has had. Those who needed a job when the current opportunity came along and particularly those whose future work options are limited are far more likely to be accepting of work-related problems. Similarly, those whose current position compares favorably to previous jobs are more likely to take work difficulties in stride. Here is the way some of them expressed it:

[A former nursing home activities director]: I saw this as an opportunity to get out of the isolated environment and get into the community in an agency program.

[A former mental health worker]: Compared to other kinds of jobs that I have had, I would say this job is relatively unstressful.... I worked in a mental health program. The public's perception of people in mental health is a lot different from the public's perception of someone who's involved in a meals program. Meals is looked at as a legitimate need, people being hungry, so I think there is a little more status being involved in this type of program. It's more acceptable, more recognized. It seems a more worthwhile service, and I have to admit that [that] feels good. You don't have to be defensive about what you're doing or always have to explain what you're doing and why it's important.

Further illustration of this form of comparison comes from a recent study of public school teachers (Fiske, 1982). The study found that men who had become teachers as a way of avoiding being sent by the military to Vietnam were among the most disaffected respondents. At one time teaching was perceived as a far more favorable undertaking than fighting a war. However, once the threat of military duty subsided, the occupation of teaching lost the advantages it initially had provided.

By way of contrast, a former frustrated service worker who had left her agency to enter the business world was interviewed. Her comparison level of the service work alternative was extremely low:

> I don't think [I'd take a service job again]. I think I'm really cut out for business.... I like wearing a jacket, and I like wearing heels, and I like sitting in on meetings with big shots in the bank. The whole thing just turns me on. There's money there, and you get decent raises. Everybody gets treated well—I feel like I am—and there's growth potential. I don't think I'd go back to a public center....

Edelwich (1980) notes that service worker dissatisfactions also arise in situations in which clients make more money than the providers, there are higher-paying jobs in the same field, or, as the respondent remarked, there is more money available in the private sector.

In order for the strategy of comparisons to be a useful stress reducer or neutralizer, it is not necessary for comparisons to be made about the particular dissatisfactions that workers experience. Some did make statements such as, "This job has less paperwork." However, any comparative assessment that enables one's current position to be rated more favorably overall can function to minimize the importance of its specific stresses.

The cognitive dissonance literature (Zajonc, 1968) sheds further light on how one comes to evaluate work favorably in the face of constant work stresses. One form of cognitive dissonance is the situation of disconfirmed expectations. If service providers enter their occupation possessing what is referred to in Chapter 2 as the professional mystique, it is likely that their high expectations regarding service work will be disconfirmed, thereby producing cognitive dissonance. The dynamics of cognitive dissonance suggest that individuals attempt to eliminate it by seeking consistency among the cognitions themselves. That can be accomplished by changing existing cognitions and verbalizing favorable attitudes toward apparently unfavorable situations. Specifically, a move toward cognitive consistency is made either by minimizing the negative features of service work, emphasizing the positive features of the occupation, as seen in the quotations above, or deliberately seeking information to maximize the differences between the present job and one's options.

Cognitive dissonance research has found, in fact, that experimental subjects put into dissonant situations do not even experience dissonance if they have no choice of being able to remove themselves from the situation. Presumably, then, service providers with limited work mobility are less likely to feel stressed by disconfirmed expectations about their work environment than will those workers with occupational alternatives. Cognitive dissonance theory also proposes, somewhat ironically, that individuals who commit themselves to a boring or tedious task for an insufficient reward will come to enjoy the task. If these propositions hold for service workers, certain perverse outcomes can occur. First, despite the conflict-ridden nature of service work and the low pay accompanying its performance, many service workers will not only absorb work stresses as a matter of routine, but will also express satisfaction with their work. Second, as this is most likely to occur among workers with marginal skills and limited mobility, an agency's most dependable employees will come to be those who are the least trained and who cannot find better jobs elsewhere.

Religious Orientation

Yet another means by which respondents ease the stresses of their work situations is through taking a religious or spiritual attitude toward their jobs. This orientation is recommended by Bryan (1981) as a way to alleviate burnout among public interest group workers. One form such an orientation takes is the use of prayer when work becomes difficult. When one respondent was asked how she attempts to resolve troublesome work situations, she remarked:

> Prayer. I pray a lot on this job, and it works out real well. . . . [Prayer] is my main staple. . . . God has really just helped me deal with those kinds of stresses. He's helped me see the lighter side of everything so that I don't get real uptight about things and can manage to deal with it in a pretty easy way.

Another form that a religious orientation toward service work takes is belief in one's work as a mission or calling. Such an attitude serves to sacralize otherwise routine and perhaps tedious service tasks (Marks, 1981; Cherniss and Krantz, n.d.). Indeed, the reader will recall from Chapter 2 that perceiving one's work as a calling is characteristic of the altruist model of service work. Such an attitude is reflected in the following comments by one of the interviewees:

> At the present time I have no dislikes in regards to the work simply because it [calls on] God-given talent. In order to succeed or to be successful at any task that is given to you by God, you present yourself [well]. Instead of me looking for what the agency and the job has to offer, I look into myself to see what I have to offer. . . . There will be hard days, . . . and these are things I've learned to cope with and like. Every day is not a bed of roses outside of your heart; it's only on the inside of the individual that it works out.

Closely related to a religious or spiritual orientation to one's work is an approach that emphasizes the power of positive thinking. Like its counterpart religious ideologies, the positive orientation serves individuals well by reducing the stresses accompanying their work. One service provider, when asked if she had ever had demands made upon her at work that caused stress or conflict, responded:

> No. I say that real fast, and, really, no. I guess it depends on the outlook I have on life and the way I look at things. I cannot afford anything to bring stress into my life. I'm too busy for it. . . . I can't afford being broken down; . . . I'm too busy trying to help other people. As long as I'm doing that, I don't have time to let other things get to me. . . . [Later, when asked what the term "occupational burnout" means to her]: Occupational burnout? To me it really doesn't mean anything because I don't ever intend to have it. . . . I wouldn't let myself.

In summary, a religious, spiritual, or positive orientation to one's work represents either a means whereby work conflicts fail to become stressful or experienced stresses are managed. These stances work favorably for a small group of the respondents.

Advocacy

A final technique reported by the interviewees for the management of work stress is the undertaking of advocacy. Advocacy efforts, designed to produce change and thereby eliminate specific work dissatisfactions, are engaged in by only a small number of providers. Here are the comments of two:

With the disappointments, that's where advocacy comes in. I have been involved in trying to assist in writing a state bill . . . that would give the state more power to enforce some regulations . . . , and that's one way of coping with it.

If we could, more of us would advocate for the elderly at the top level in terms of working with legislators and the power structure, those folks who are making the decisions. I think maybe sometimes as people in direct services, we do not advocate enough. We do not get as involved in trying to deal with the problem and the guidelines before they become the rules and the regulations. . . . But if we had enough people getting involved and trying to deal with these problems, I think there could be some changes.

Based on the arguments in Chapters 3 and 4, it follows that of all of the techniques utilized to manage the stresses of service work, advocacy has the chance to produce the most significant effects because it acknowledges the impact of larger systems on workers' problems. This claim does not deny certain shortcomings that may characterize advocacy efforts:

[A]dvocacy perpetuates the "worker as savior" myth, regardless of its underlying good will. It rests on the assumption that the sources of accumulated wealth and power will be responsive to requests or demands from the social worker in a way that will lead to fundamental change. It is . . . based on the liberal concern for the deprivation of others, rather than the oppression of all, and on a continued belief in the potential of the existing system to be responsive, if only the correct approach can be found. . . . (Galper, 1975:133)

This concern and the prospects for meaningful advocacy will be addressed in Chapter 6.

In sum, most workers employ personal or interpersonal stress-reduction techniques to cope with their difficult work situations. Indeed, most researchers on work stress and burnout suggest personal and interpersonal stress management strategies. What these researchers imply, and what service providers' behaviors convey, is that service workers are responsible, if not for the causes of stress or burnout, at least for its alleviation in their everyday lives (Karger, 1981). At best, changes introduced by service providers or administrators might rectify some troublesome situations. This analysis, however, locates primary sources of worker dissatisfactions well beyond the individual and the agency. If the arguments are correct, then the alleviation of service worker discontents calls for more far-reaching changes in the nature and conduct of human services in order to arrest the stressful conditions highlighted. The strategy of advocacy is the only one of those described that begins to address work troubles in relation to larger issues.

Conceptualizing work problems at social psychological or administrative levels when their major sources lie in larger systems allows for only short-lived amelioration and the need for ongoing attention to recurrent problems. This is not to deny that some instances of individual burnout will find their solutions in planned time-outs, mixed case loads, support systems, and like strategies; rather, it is to emphasize those many burnout experiences that are structurally induced. In the latter case, to expect that the worker will be permanently rejuvenated by one-time, individualized interventions merely structures the situation for further work stress.

So long as the discontents service workers express have their roots in the larger social areas previously identified, the potential for burnout is an ongoing hazard of the service work place. As such, the phenomenon of burnout takes on a new meaning. Insofar as the social policies workers implement are designed foremost for the benefit of politicians and the larger social order, then the discouragement, pessimism, and fatalism that are symptoms of burnout may be a realistic assessment by service workers of the situations in which they are immersed. In contrast, many writers describe these as irrational attitudes caused by work exhaustion or personal inadequacies.

In their own efforts to overcome service work stresses, providers typically turn inward to their own resources or limit themselves to seeking support or change within their own work settings. In effect, they allow public issues that are political and social in nature to become their own personal troubles. Why this is so, and what consequences it has for them, their clients, the work setting, and the welfare enterprise are addressed next.

THE CONSEQUENCES OF STRESS MANAGEMENT

Before detailing the results of the particular coping mechanisms utilized by service providers to manage stress in their work, it might be useful to try to understand how workers come to employ the techniques they do. In other words, it should be asked why service workers focus primarily on personalized ways to alleviate tensions and problems when it has been argued that the problems they encounter have significant nonpersonal origins.

One of the reasons for this discrepancy lies in the manner in which individuals generally construct the reality around them. The personal worlds in which people live are typically ones that "are limited to the close-up scenes of job, family, neighborhood" (Mills, 1959:3). The farther the imaginations are extended beyond these boundaries, the more difficult it becomes to make sense of larger dynamics or one's place within them. This feeling is exacerbated by the rapid pace of social and technological change and the proliferation of bureaucratic organization. Perhaps as self-defense from a world that appears overwhelming, people withdraw into personalized microworlds. That is, realities are constructed, difficulties included, in individualized terms, not in terms of the larger institutions or the historical dynamics of which one is a part. The result is the transformation of public issues into personal troubles, along with a limited vision of how these might be resolved.

Another reason for the discrepancy between the source of problems and the solutions employed lies in a paradox. It has been noted already that advocacy on the part of service providers— their becoming politicized and seeking social change—is the coping mechanism most likely to produce permanent alleviation of work conflicts. Yet, the action of advocacy requires an even greater commitment to their jobs than they currently exhibit. In other words, it demands an increase in the amount of time and energy devoted to work-related roles and activities, notwithstanding the already intense demands on workers' time and energy. To expect service workers to commit themselves to action for social change is tantamount to expecting them to exacerbate the pressures they presently experience. According to Cherniss (1980:134), "there is some evidence that these individuals [who seek to bring about social and institutional change through their work] experience more job stress than others." Thus, the already heavy demands on service personnel mitigate against the likelihood that they will expand their responsibilities to include advocacy.

The personal and professional orientations of many of the workers interviewed also operate to decrease the likelihood of advocacy. Many view the central task of their jobs as direct interaction with, and the provision of assistance to, their clients. As Trattner (1979) notes, the professionalization of social service work resulted in a casework approach rather than collective action for social change. The more professional a service worker becomes, the more likely that individual is committed to casework as the appropriate orientation to service delivery. Any activity that takes time away from this responsibility, such as paperwork, meetings, conferences, and advocacy will be viewed negatively by these providers. Accordingly, their commitment to action for social change is likely to be low.

Even if a service worker's orientation is activist and collective, the service organization's orientation to individualized client casework can exert strong influence on the way that providers carry out their work. This argument is reinforced by the findings from Robin and Wagenfeld's (1977) study of community mental health workers. Workers who expressed a high activist orientation to their work scored high on role discrepancy; that is, strong disagreement existed between these workers and their employers regarding the definition of their work role. Role discrepancy is highest among workers employed the shortest amount of time and declines noticeably the longer one is employed within the organization. Presumably, employees come to adapt to the orientation of their agency rather than persist in the activist perspective they brought to the job. Insofar as agencies are not supportive of action for social change, it seems unrealistic to expect that orientation to persist or prevail among its employees.

One further reason that workers may not seek political or regulatory change is that certain changes may be even more disliked than the present arrangements. A case in point is the writer's experience in conducting a workshop for service providers on the dysfunctions of age-specific policies. It was noted in that session that one way of reducing large caseloads and their accompanying frustrations is to limit the client pool through the introduction of means testing for services. This proved to be an unpopular alternative for workers in attendance because, they argued, it would

(a) require time spent in determining eligibility, (b) increase paperwork demands, (c) restrict their discretion in choice of clients, and (d) undermine the political momentum built around the provision of services and programs to all older Americans, regardless of income or severity of need.

In sum, for social psychological, structural, and political reasons, it is not surprising that many service providers turn the public issues of their work into their own personal troubles. Nevertheless, their personalized responses to work problems have consequences that are social and political, as well as personal, in nature.

Consequences for Service Providers

The most immediate consequence derived by service providers from the stress management strategies they employ is being able to get by in their work. Certain coping strategies function to enable one to take problems in stride (as do religious orientations and comparisons); they make lowered job performance acceptable (as do limited expectations, the prioritizing of tasks, detached concern, negative feelings for the client, and appeals to biology); they give one respite from work-related roles (as do compartmentalization, the abridging of role relationships, delegation, and extension); or they make sense out of confusing and disorderly situations (as do the quasi theories of time and communication).

In sum, short-term and temporary resolution of work-related problems is the likely outcome. Once relief is achieved, workers are temporarily renewed to return to the stress-filled work environment until once again they must employ these techniques to avoid feeling completely overwhelmed by their work. Insofar as these coping strategies become institutionalized, workers will have come to adapt to the inadequacies of the service system in which they are employed.

One concern about the utilization of such coping mechanisms, specifically conversations and gripe sessions with coworkers, is that these will serve the latent function of "draining off and deflecting the worker's need for a more formally organized, systematic approach to his problem as a worker in a bureaucracy" (Wasserman, 1971:95). A second concern is that, because the priority of workers is likely to be on the alignment of their behavior with the requirements of the work setting, the profession's service ideals will be displaced and eventually transformed (Stokes and Hewitt, 1976). In fact, Zajonc (1968) provides the basis for arguing that service worker attitudes will be altered along with service ideals. He notes that settings that restrict behavioral responses make conformity to those settings more likely. If verbalizations come into play that argue on behalf of the conforming behaviors, as noted with the use of accounts, then private attitude change will likely accompany public behavioral conformity. Thus, service providers will come to believe in and endorse those attitudes and behaviors they initially introduced into their work repertoire as coping devices against work stress. The result of these dynamics is a service ideology quite removed from the altruist model described in Chapter 2.

How do the findings speak to the existence of the variant models of service work introduced at the outset? Do service providers resemble the altruist or the dirty worker? Does the applicability of these models change over the course of the service work career? From this study, as well as from other available data, it is reasonable to argue that human service workers may embody both orientations simultaneously. On the one hand, the *personal stance* of many of the interviewees toward the people aspects of their work is one of sincere concern. Regardless of the specific troubles of the work setting, most of the respondents derive pleasure from helping people. These pieces of the service worker puzzle fit the altruist model. On the other hand, the *role enactment* of these same providers reinforces the images of the dirty worker model. This model becomes manifest in service workers' strategies of role manipulation and role bargaining and in the inability or unwillingness of most to challenge an inadequate service system and/or the policies guiding it. By virtue of trying to cope with their own problems, service workers unintentionally reinforce arrangements from which both they and their clients stand to lose. The best guess is that the longer service providers remain in stress-producing service systems, the more likely it is that their attitudes will become aligned with work requirements. In turn, the more likely it is that the dirty worker model will come to prevail.

Consequences for the Client

The effects on clients from service workers' strategies for stress management are varied, depending on the particular devices used. From workers who employ religion and favorable comparisons, the client is likely to notice little change in the provider-client role relationship over time (e.g., Cherniss and Krantz, n.d.). With employees who use role bargaining to reduce the demands of their work, the client is likely to sense distraction or disinterest. At worst, the client may experience hostility and abuse from those who cope through norm violations. Providers who emphasize role manipulation for stress reduction will create a discontinuity of role partners for the client; that is, the client cannot expect attention from the same individual throughout the service experience or from the same person at any time of the day because of the provider's use of compartmentalization, time-outs, delegation of tasks, and extension of other responsibilities. Collectively, high employee turnover rates within an agency may lead to further client experiences of discontinuous or inconsistent attention.

On the favorable side, service providers who cope by trying to stretch guidelines may be able to offer discretionary assistance to some clients who otherwise might not have been eligible for benefits or services. However, such behaviors are client-specific; that is, service providers can withhold or implement this option based on their personal assessment of the client. Insofar as certain types of clients (e.g., middle class, articulate, responsive) are preferred over others, only some clients can expect to benefit from the use of this coping strategy (Street et al., 1979).

Finally, clients will be affected categorically by political efforts undertaken by service workers to change the parameters of their work. Resultant changes in service policies or practices may or may not benefit the client, as seen in the next chapter. In some cases decisions that help the service worker perform his/her job more easily or efficiently have deleterious effects on the nature of the provider-client relationship or the quality of the service provided. On the other hand, decisions intended to enhance the service experience for the client may function to increase demands on service workers or complicate the execution of their job.

Consequences for the Service Agency

Just as the effects of workers' coping strategies are varied in relation to the client, so are they variable in their impact on service agencies. The overall effects on any particular agency will be determined by the particular configuration of coping devices utilized by that agency's workers.

In agencies where role manipulation is a preferred technique, absenteeism and turnover may be high. While absenteeism will put additional strain on available workers, a certain amount is not necessarily dysfunctional for an agency, especially if it allows employees to return refreshed. Neither is turnover, within reason, necessarily a problem. In fact, employee resignations may rid the agency of burned out or low-functioning workers who can be replaced by fresher individuals.

Role bargaining and norm violation can be troublesome for a service agency. Insofar as the former leads to low-level performance on the job and the latter takes the form of client neglect or abuse, agencies are vulnerable to criticism. Further, in times of funding cutbacks when service organizations are being expected to do more with less, agencies whose workers cope by role bargaining cannot anticipate fulfilling that new demand.

One form of role bargaining that works in the agency's favor, however, is priority setting among a host of responsibilities. While priority setting is, in part, a matter of personal preference, it also is related to the relative power of the role partners with whom the worker interacts (Goode, 1960). Given the discussion in Chapter 3 of the pulls on service providers from both clients and the employer, along with an understanding of their relative power, it is expected that workers' priorities will place their employers' needs over clients' needs. As a consequence, any negative functions of priority setting fall disproportionately on clients and the quality or quantity of services they receive and work in favor of the accomplishment of internal organizational tasks.

The use of quasi theories by workers also has implications for service agencies. In agencies whose workers employ the quasi theory of time, it may be possible to ignore problems as they emerge and attend only to those that persist at high levels of annoyance. This should make the burdens of supervisors and managers lighter. On the other hand, administrators whose workers adhere to the quasi-theory of communication will be pressed to institute formal procedures to sound out and converse with workers at all levels. Formalized channels of communication may be an inexpensive way of maintaining worker morale, regardless of whether it resolves other work problems. On the other hand, it could provide the vehicle through which dissatisfactions become contagious among workers (Edelwich, 1980), thereby exacerbating agency problems.

Finally, agencies will be able to maintain some degree of worker satisfaction in situations where workers compare their present jobs favorably to other possibilities. In times of retrenchment when worker mobility is limited, administrators may not have significant concern with this issue. However, when services are expanding, or when valued employees locate occupational alternatives even in slack times, it behooves administrators to take certain actions that allow their agencies to be compared favorably against other work settings and occupational alternatives. These actions might be symbolic or material, depending on particular workers' valued rewards. Insofar as administrators are unable or unwilling to respond in such a manner, they can expect employee turnover to occur.

Consequences for the Welfare Enterprise

It is not stretching a point to argue that the coping behaviors of service providers have significant consequences for the entire enterprise of social welfare. Lipsky (1978:397) maintains that

> where considerable discretion characterizes the jobs of people who imple-
> ment public-agency activities, people "make" policy in hidden concert
> with others in similar positions through their patterned responses to the
> situations and circumstances in which they find themselves.

Mills (1959:3) writes, as well, that "[t]he facts of contemporary history are also facts about the success and the failure of individual men and women." The ways in which the interviewees execute their work responsibilities, and the ways in which similar kinds of roles are performed in one service setting after another, contribute to social welfare policymaking (Pressman and Wildavsky, 1979). What, then, are some of the consequences for the conduct of social welfare that flow from the particular coping strategies utilized to reduce work stress?

One likely outcome is the persistence of the most serious conflicts and contradictions of service work despite the use of diverse coping strategies. Work problems will not be alleviated because the implicit analysis of problem sources is inadequate; the typical coping techniques used, with the possible exception of advocacy, only alleviate the symptoms of larger problems on a temporary basis.

Internal contradictions are an inherent characteristic of welfare work. To the extent that ongoing frustrations from these contradictions lead service providers to reassess their clients and their jobs negatively, the segment of the public that devalues and stigmatizes service recipients and social welfare undertakings will be reinforced (e.g., Scott, 1967b). Indeed, the constructions of reality that frustrated service workers develop and disseminate as firsthand observers of the social welfare enterprise can serve as ready ammunition for those groups who favor reduced public assistance. Further, to the extent that public goodwill toward welfare activities erodes, so will political sentiment. In these instances, the retrenchment of social welfare services or the alteration of social welfare policy toward a more punitive orientation is likely to be seen. In essence, clients become the scapegoats for service workers' problems that are structural and political in nature; the decision makers whose policies generate welfare difficulties are buffered from criticism.

Another likely outcome involves the resolution of social work ideals with the actual conduct of helping people. Given discrepancies between the ideal of altruism and the nature of service performance in the real world, which will exert more influence in the long run? The use of verbal aligning actions, or statements that uphold service ideals in the face of provider conduct at variance with those ideals, pays lip service to the cultural expectations of altruism in the service provider role. As such, cultural ideals can be maintained. However, Stokes and Hewitt (1976:848) contend that, over the long run, variant conduct serves as an instigator of social change and that "the evolutionary drift is toward the adjustment of culture to actual conduct." Thus, service worker coping strategies may contribute to the institutionalization of limited work involvement by service personnel and the emergence of a very different ideal of social work than the model of altruism. Indeed, it has already been argued that the dirty worker model prevails, de facto, over time in individual service work careers.

In short, the routinized conduct that ordinary service providers employ (*see* Friedman, 1974) to adapt to work stresses has serious implications for larger social welfare dynamics. At first glance, workers' coping mechanisms appear to work for them on a temporary basis. At worst, they seem to generate minor skirmishes with clients or coworkers. However, put into their larger context, these adaptive behaviors serve to transform the role of altruist to that of dirty worker, erode public support for welfare functions, and perpetuate an inadequate social welfare system.

Chapter 6

THE FUTURE OF SERVICE WORK
Is There a Way Out of the Service Trap?

In the preceding chapters, several points have been developed. First, the work of today's human service providers is so riddled with tensions, conflicts, and frustrations that the simple image of the service worker as humanitarian agent is naive and misleading at best. Second, many of the problems encountered by these personnel in the day-to-day execution of their work derive from areas well beyond their everyday experiences: problems originate in the dynamics of organizational life, political activity, and public opinion. Third, in their attempts to manage their daily difficulties, service providers develop personalized coping strategies that alleviate stress in the short term but that in the longer run serve to perpetuate welfare system inadequacies. In effect, service workers become trapped by their own adaptive behaviors.

This chapter addresses the question, Is there a way out of the service trap? Before doing so, it will first examine how significant changes at the federal level with respect to the human services will exacerbate service worker problems. Then it will assess the utility of various social welfare proposals for improving the plight of service personnel and their clients and, by implication, for renewing the social welfare enterprise.

THE IMPACT OF RECENT INITIATIVES

Significant initiatives are occurring at the federal level of government that are destined, if fully implemented, to have profound impact on social welfare institutions and their personnel. The major initiatives discussed here are federal responses to the fiscal crisis and the emergence of the new federalism. The broad outlines of each of these directions are briefly described and their demonstrated, or likely impact on the work of public service providers is discussed. The overriding theme of the following discussion is that, on balance, the actual and proposed changes will make the everyday tasks of service workers even more difficult than has already been described.

Fiscal Crisis

A major theme brewing at the state level for the past decade and underlying Ronald Reagan's election to the presidency is the perceived (if not real) unwillingness of taxpayers to underwrite additional governmental social spending. Governments at all levels have been admonished to balance their budgets and to get government out of the pockets of the citizenry. The concern here is not to debate whether the country's present fiscal state deserves the crisis label; that is, it does not focus on the extent to which the crisis definition is objective (e.g., O'Connor, 1973) or subjective (e.g., Edelman, 1977). The state of crisis may exist as a real condition of the political economy, or it may be manufactured for certain political purposes. The purpose is to describe what measures have been or are likely to be taken as a result of popular or political acceptance of the crisis definition, whatever its origin.

Prior to discussing the impact of fiscal difficulties on human service work, several qualifications need to be made. First, a popular means of describing budgetary actions related to human services is through the use of the phrase "funding cuts." As Rose (1980) notes, however, such terminology creates misperceptions of governmental actions. In fact,

> [w]hichever criterion is used—current or constant money or both—current political and academic discussion of "cuts" in public expenditure is inconsistent with aggregate evidence. (Rose, 1980:210)

Indeed, total public expenditures in the United States have increased in the 1960s, 1970s, and 1980s. What is popularly referred to as cutbacks often reflects one of the following conditions instead: (a) expenditures that grow at a lower rate than they have historically, (b) expenditures that grow at a lower rate than previously announced commitments had promised, or (c) expenditures that increase in current money terms but decrease in constant value, creating a spending squeeze (Rose, 1980).

A second point regarding the discussion of the fiscal crisis is that different social programs and regions of the country are differentially impacted by the situation. While the discussion focuses on impacts in general, the reader must be cognizant that service programs and personnel are unequally affected depending on such factors as whether they operate in cities, rural areas, or suburban areas, whether they are located in Sunbelt or Frostbelt regions, what specific clientele they serve, and how long personnel have worked in a particular service position. As a general guideline, it is reasonable to presume that workers in inner cities of Frostbelt states or rural areas in the Sunbelt states serving the most devalued populations will be hardest hit by the fiscal crisis (Muller, 1982). Similarly, those workers with the least tenure in the workplace are likely to be disproportionately affected; in many instances these will be members of minority groups (Peters, 1980).

Third, discussion of the retrenchment of social programs as a means of addressing the nation's fiscal stress is focused for the most part on items deemed controllable, or discretionary expenditures. Service personnel who work with programs that fall into this category are likely to bear disproportionate burdens of retrenchment. The so-called uncontrollable spending items are "those that are committed by statute or contract" by the government (Rose, 1980:222) and have been referred to by politicians and the public as "entitlement programs." These include Social Security retirement benefits, food stamps, AFDC, unemployment compensation, veterans' benefits, and the like, along with the cost of interest on the public debt. The federal government estimates that these relatively uncontrollable items constitute roughly 75 percent of governmental expenditures (Rose, 1980; Peters, 1980; Schick, 1980). Consequently, only about one-fourth of the federal budget is readily amenable to adjustments; the programs within that portion of the budget will be hardest hit during times of retrenchment. Indeed, if spending trends for federal grants-in-aid to states and localities, which reflect the bulk of discretionary social program spending (e.g., Title XX Social Security Act social services, Older Americans Act programs, job training and placement activities) are looked at, actual declines in constant dollar allocations beginning in 1978 and deepening in the subsequent fiscal years can be seen (Beam and Colella, 1980). This does not deny the fact that much tinkering is being undertaken with the regulations and formulae of entitlement programs as well; rather, the point is that the severest effects from an agency standpoint will be felt in discretionary social programs.

Having made these qualifications, the actual and likely impacts of the fiscal crisis as they relate to direct service provision will be discussed. The clearest impact that the appeal for a balanced budget or a smaller annual federal deficit has had on human services is in the level of available funding. As previously noted, reduced funding may take the form of a spending squeeze or an actual cut in discretionary programs or, less drastically, a reduction of expected increases for entitlement programs. For example, it is estimated that federal funding for the Administration on Aging and for Title XX Social Services, the two primary funding sources for programs administered by the workers interviewed, would be reduced by 27 percent and 43 percent respectively, from 1981 to 1983 (in Gutowski and Koshel, 1982; Table 10-2).

Specific administrative responses to these reductions are associated with, and exacerbate, the problems experienced by service personnel. After exhausting various stopgap measures such as depleting existing surpluses, engaging in interfund borrowing, or improving purchasing procedures (Wolman, 1980; Fosler, 1980), administrators are likely to realize savings through a reduction in staff by attrition or layoffs and an emphasis on greater efficiency and productivity for those remaining. In other words, service workers will be asked to do more with less, thereby exacerbating their already pervasive feeling of lack of time for proper attention to clients. Not only will they be expected to perform their usual tasks, but also to take on some of the responsibilities of workers whose positions are eliminated or frozen. This circumstance is likely to heighten workers' perceptions of ambiguity regarding their precise job responsibilities and associated priorities (Lipsky, 1980).

With funding reductions, clients may have to become more

demanding in order to obtain increasingly scarce services. Such demands may take the form of increasing use of the emergency label in order to capture the worker's attention from among a host of competing clientele. Situations such as this will further reduce service providers' control over the worker-client relationship or function to harden the worker to clients' descriptions of the urgency of their need.

Administrative emphasis on efficiency and productivity in the face of retrenchment at first may take the forms of improved scheduling, work reorganization, the use of new technology including data processing systems, improved matching of the work force to the workload, and task reassignment for optimal use of worker skills (Wolman, 1980; Fosler, 1980). Any or all of these strategies can contribute to cost savings that can be measured quantitatively. It is difficult at best, however, to develop and require strategies to make service workers more efficient and productive in the qualitative dimensions of their jobs, that is, in areas of relationship to the client. Any attempt to institute such procedures is likely to enhance the already strong feeling that there is not enough time to manage one's current caseload in a caring or humanitarian way. Even to discuss increased productivity with regard to human relationships is anathema to providers with strong client-centered service work orientations.

To summarize thus far, an immediate predictable response by service organizations to funding reductions is to exploit various stopgap measures for the short term and to increase technical efficiency as much as possible. Beyond that, a reduction in the work force through attrition or layoffs achieves cost savings, and the remaining staff is expected to carry greater responsibilities than in the past. These measures have the effect of cutting spending without cutting services.

If such measures are inadequate to balance budgets, at some point the decision to reduce services is made. This decision, like that of staff cutbacks, is characterized by patterned responses that heighten worker problems. In the short term, the most likely response by administrators to the need to cut services is to make across-the-board cuts (Beam and Colella, 1980; Wolman, 1980). This means that all programs have to sacrifice a certain percentage of their budget. While equal sacrifice has certain political appeal, this strategy will not be well received by providers who view their own programs as having foremost importance and impact. In fact, across-the-board reductions may be seen as unfair punishment for programs that excel and unjust reprieve for programs that have not proven so successful.

Prolonged fiscal stress eventually leads to selective program reductions rather than across-the-board cuts (Wolman, 1980). Selective reductions require each agency or program to wage a serious campaign to retain existing funding levels. To do this, staff members must be mobilized for political lobbying efforts. This responsibility, along with new duties gained due to staff vacancies or reductions, further strains workers' capacities to meet all work demands. As a result, role bargaining is likely to occur to an even greater extent than it currently does.

Whether cuts come across-the-board or selectively, they strengthen workers' existing complaints about the lack of funds to provide services adequately or fully. They operate more subtly, as well. When services contract, they put the provider in the position of having to say no more often to potential beneficiaries. In doing so, providers undermine the primary reason that many entered service work, that is, to help others. This can be a cause of reduction in worker morale.

Two of the most visible and predictable responses to fiscal retrenchment in human services have been noted: cutting staff and cutting services. Other less visible reactions and their consequences for service providers should be acknowledged as well. First, retrenchment takes the form of a reduction in operating budgets. Along with retrenchment comes a host of new regulations regarding cuts, thereby adding to workers' burdens of accountability and its accompanying paperwork requirements.

Second, any new programs initiated in response to constituent demands are bound to be small (Beam and Colella, 1980) and are likely to be developed sporadically and unsystematically (Schick, 1980). The first characteristic sets up provider frustrations from the outset because new programs will be token activities at best, with high expectations but with minimal funds. New programs that incur low initial costs but whose costs escalate in later years will only delay provider frustrations, while allowing more time for client expectations to be raised beyond what can be delivered. The likelihood that new programs will not be coordinated with existing ones requires that its new workers spend great effort articulating it with ongoing activities and that existing agency workers incorporate it into the service scenario. Both of these requirements are time-consuming endeavors that at least temporarily take away from the direct service effort.

Third, considerable controversy has been generated by a proposed constitutional amendment to require a balanced federal budget. This requirement may be useful as a political or economic planning tool; however, if a balanced budget amendment were passed, the ambiguities under which service providers now work are likely to be heightened. In effect, the current budgeting process is stretched out over sixteen months prior to the beginning of a fiscal year, during which time various scenarios of income and expenditures are utilized to predict program allocations. The requirement of a balanced budget would extend the process to twenty-eight months and provide less latitude within which decision makers could operate in making allocations, especially in the latter quarters of the fiscal year. This would cause program administrators to be even more fiscally conservative than they are presently and broaden the gap in spending perspectives between line staff and agency executives. Further, if large shortfalls of income had to be made up in the final quarters of a year, budget cuts would have to be far more drastic than they are at present. (*See* Nordhaus [1981] and Senior Citizens News [1982] for further effects of instituting a mandated balanced budget.)

In sum, reductions in the federal budget for human services have, or can be expected to, set in motion even greater problems in all four areas of complaint registered by service workers in Chapter 2.

If service personnel are disadvantaged with regard to the actualities of fiscal retrenchment, they also stand to lose in terms of the rhetoric of the crisis. Many providers will adjust their work behaviors in order to maintain quality services to clients, perhaps at some personal cost to themselves. In doing so, however, service workers become the shock absorbers of service system retrenchment and provide funding sources with justifications for their reduction of funds. If providers accomplish at least as much with less funding, they lend credence to the claim that cutbacks eliminate waste, duplication, fat, and fraud without harming the social safety net of assistance. Although providers might be victims of retrenchment, their adjustments to retrenchment backfire on them. It becomes easy to blame them for a previously extravagant or "fat" welfare system. To be sure, social workers in Great Britain have been perceived in this manner as severe cuts have been made in that country's social services (*see* Specht's [1981] review of Brewer and Lait [1980]).

A great deal of attention has been devoted to ways for service administrators to make up for financial shortfalls. Three specific remedies that have been put forth by politicians and providers alike are (1) greater reliance on private sector contributions to fund services, (2) greater reliance on the use of volunteers to substitute for reductions in staff, and (3) greater use of client copayments for services they receive. The evidence regarding the degree to which these strategies are effective is not promising. It is unlikely that these measures will adequately fill the voids created by reduction in federal support for human services.

Morris (1982:338) concludes that business contributions to nonprofit service organizations will not significantly relieve funding shortfalls:

> In the last year, major business corporations provided . . . less than 5 percent of the amount contributed by nongovernmental sources. Only a quarter of the nation's corporations make donations to charity at all, and these tend to average about 1 percent of taxable income.

In a recent survey of the nation's business executives, The Conference Board, a business research institute, found that fully 60 percent of the businesses surveyed "plan only normal increases in their charity budgets this year." Only 6 percent planned increases in direct response to reductions in federal spending (Broadway, 1982:1D). Among the constraints on corporate giving are various legal mandates regarding where such contributions can be directed (Morris, 1982), the reluctance by some businesses to make what are, in effect, social welfare decisions, and the existence of corporations' own fiscal problems in recessionary times (Broadway, 1982).

Fund raising from the general public does not appear to be an adequate solution, either. While private individuals gave approximately $40 billion to nonprofit organizations in 1980, over half of that went to nonwelfare church activities (Morris, 1982). Bergmann (1981) notes that individuals may be reluctant to make contributions because their donation is unlikely to have meaningful impact. Further, she cites a major problem with voluntary collections: some collection organizations spend in excess of 90 percent of the money collected to wage and manage the solicitation campaign itself. Thus, what funds do reach human service agencies are sharply reduced in relation to the campaign's fund-raising goal. Even if private giving expanded significantly, it is unlikely that it could compensate for the more than 50 percent share of the budget of nonprofit social welfare organizations that has been derived from the federal government. Salamon and Abramson (1982) report that private giving would have to increase more than fourfold through 1985 in order to fill the funding gaps left by federal reductions. Such a boost may prove illusory in light of the previous record annual increase of only 12 percent and in light of new tax laws that increase the cost of contributions, especially for upper-income taxpayers. Finally, dissatisfactions are reported with funding from collective community charities such as the United Way. Funds from this source are accompanied by large amounts of paperwork and "too much control for too little money" (Netting, 1982:594), making their acceptance costly from an administrative standpoint.

A second remedy for funding shortfalls is the use of volunteers to fill gaps left by staff reductions. Certain problems exist with this argument, as well. While expectations have been raised, the usual pool of community service volunteers, middle-aged women, has declined due to their growing rate of participation in the labor force. Further, there are some tasks that cannot be done by volunteers because of various rules or licensing requirements (Fraley, 1982). Even if volunteers are acquired to fill part of the gap in staffing, additional time of paid staff is required to coordinate and oversee the activities of the volunteer service providers.

The third measure for diminishing the impact of reductions is the use of client contributions or copayments (e.g., "State and local AAA's," 1982). Services previously provided free will instead seek donations from recipients, as in the case of congregate meals programs for the elderly, or require partial payment for certain goods, as in the case of copayments for prescriptions filled through Medicaid. The revenues from copayments will not offset funding reductions; they will only make their impact less severe. Arguments against the copayments strategy include the concerns that (a) it will drive away those clients who may need services the most and (b) the various regulations surrounding copayments can be more costly to administer than the revenues they produce (Seabrook, 1982).

In short, the fiscal crisis exacerbates the difficulties service providers experience in less recessionary times; responses to the crisis to date have not proven to be adequate remedies for alleviating those difficulties. In effect, service personnel are the less visible victims of reduction in support for social service activities. Edelwich (1980:33) writes that

> it is not surprising that people have become conscious of it [burnout] — and given it a name—in the 1970's. Although the strain on the individual worker was just as great in the 1960's as it is today, enthusiasm probably lasted longer when there was a hopeful sense that society supported the idea of helping the less fortunate. That commitment was backed up by increased outlay of funds which made the human services an expanding enterprise. Today, with those funds being reclaimed . . . , the enthusiasm of the 1960's has burned out. For on top of the concrete practical difficulties created by reductions in funding, the very idea of a "taxpayers' revolt" against human services funding is necessarily dispiriting to those who staff the agencies under attack.

The New Federalism

Although the new federalism is not all that new, it is a concept whose visibility and impact accelerated under President Reagan. Simply stated, the new federalism is the most recent attempt to clarify the division of labor between states and the federal government regarding responsibility for social welfare and community improvement activities. Closely linked to the fiscal crisis, the new federalism is also an effort to get states to assume programs and services that the fiscally beleaguered federal government had initiated (Weisman, 1982). The original broad scheme for the new federalism involved states taking over all of the costs of AFDC, food stamps, and numerous other programs in the areas of transportation, health and nutrition, energy assistance, education and training, revenue sharing, and community development. In return, Washington would assume full Medicaid obligations and establish a temporary trust fund that would provide states short-term assistance with their new fiscal responsibilities. Later versions of the plan have altered the original details considerably (e.g., Peterson, 1982).

The response to this proposal by state governors has been ambivalent (e.g., Ayres, 1981; Clymer, 1982; Herbers, 1982a; Pear, 1982). On the one hand, they are anxious for states to have greater programmatic flexibility than they have had under federal programs; on the other hand, they have serious reservations about the states' fiscal ability to shoulder the new responsibilities, even with temporary federal financial assistance. Nor are they anxious to shift "the pain of visible public failure . . . to [their] level of government" (Pressman and Wildavsky, 1979:170).

In order to understand the impact of the new federalism on direct service providers, it is first necessary to address two questions: (a) Do states have the capacity to undertake large social welfare responsibilities? (b) Should states be the primary initiators of social service activities? An earlier chapter noted that a major reason the federal government became so heavily involved in welfare issues originally was the inability or unwillingness of the states to maintain their own populations adequately or justly. In the 1980s are they any more capable of shouldering this responsibility?

Conclusions about these questions are mixed. From a structural standpoint, "[s]tate governments . . . have vastly improved both their capacity to govern and their sensitivity to public need" (Herbers, 1981:1) by undergoing reapportionment, strengthening gubernatorial powers, diversifying their tax bases, and assuming various service responsibilities from cities, towns, and counties. These changes make them far more capable of discharging new federalism initiatives now than previously. On the other hand, the extent of these improvements varies from state to state. Some state legislatures still do not have the available staff and expertise to make informed decisions on complex welfare issues (Herbers, 1981). Also, a shift to state decision making about social programs would represent a shift of power from the cities to the suburbs: state governments tend to be dominated by suburban interests, whereas the federal government has evinced particular concern for the nation's cities (Wade, 1982). How this shift of power would impact welfare decisions is unclear.

From a fiscal standpoint, the answer to the question of whether or not states can assume greater welfare responsibilities is more clear-cut. That answer invariably is negative, unless significant changes occur either in the form of increased revenues or program reductions. The shift of responsibility for various social programs from the federal government to the states has been accompanied by substantial funding cuts from Washington for these programs. States are assuming federal programs but with reduced allocations for operating them. In effect, then, the states are bearing the burden of making the tough cutback decisions mandated by reduced federal funding in order to carry out their end of the new federalism initiative. In numerous cases, they have not had the decision-making flexibility that the rhetoric of new federalism promised. Rather, various strings attached to block grants have prevented state legislators and administrators from making independent decisions about the programs passed down to them. These difficulties have produced the claim that the new federalism looks good, so long as one is viewing it from Washington and not from the state capitol (Ayres, 1981).

The outlook for states to make up for reduced federal funds through state and local revenues is not favorable. In the first place, neither level of government can generate adequate revenues for social spending as long as profits of the private sector remain largely untapped (*see* O'Connor, 1973). Second, there appears to be a growing popular and political resistance to further taxation, represented most visibly by Proposition 13 sentiments from taxpayers. At least twenty-five states have enacted various limits on taxing and spending since 1976 (Peterson, 1982). Still, the property tax is being used as a last resort for new local revenue production, according to a recent survey of 301 cities (Herbers, 1982b). By the 1983 fiscal year a majority of states had to raise certain taxes, even on the heels of an era of tax relief (Peterson, 1982; "Federal spending up", 1983). Further revenue difficulty arises because of states' restrictions on the types and rates of taxation that local governments can undertake. Local governments typically must depend on property, sales, and excise taxes that do not grow as rapidly as income taxes (Peters, 1980). A fourth revenue constraint derives from competition among states and localities for new residents and industry, leading them to keep a lid on taxation that ordinarily could produce additional revenues for social programs (Peters, 1980). Finally, state budgeting tends to be more conservative and limited in perspective (O'Connor, 1973), making state-level decision makers less likely than their national counterparts to invest in human service programs. One state legislator noted, for example, that it is politically easier to cut services to the poor because they do not have an active constituency at the state level and to use funds instead for crime fighting, which his constituents support (Herbers, 1982c). A survey by the Urban Institute on states' responses to the issue of replacement funding concluded: (a) that state funding replacement has been low; (b) that while social service programs have experienced the highest rates of replacement, such replacement has been small and selective; and (c) that the state's fiscal condition, and not its history of spending on human services, seems to be the most important short-term predictor of willingness to undertake replacement funding (Peterson, 1982).

Finally, the questions of states' capabilities and appropriateness for welfare initiatives must be addressed from theoretical and philosophical perspectives. The rhetoric of the new federalism claims that decisions will be brought closer to the people who are affected by them. This argument has a certain populist appeal. A 1981 Gallup poll found that a majority of respondents believe that state governments are both more understanding of peoples' needs and more efficient in conducting programs to meet those needs than is the national government (Peterson, 1982). Further, new federalism, it is argued, has the Constitution on its side in the form of the Tenth Amendment, which reserves for the states powers not delegated to the national government (e.g., Greenhouse, 1982).

A more critical stance toward enhanced state responsibility, however, includes the following concerns. The most basic issue is whether or not the state is the appropriate unit to shoulder social welfare responsibilities. A central argument against large state welfare responsibilities is the contention that social welfare problems are typically not created by state actions but by national trends; consequently, their solutions should not be confined within state boundaries. Harris (1953:468–9) observed over three decades ago that

> [w]hatever political validity the doctrine of states' rights may have had in the formative period of the union has been lost in the transition of the American economy from a simple and decentralized agrarian and commercial order, in which the individual or family was the economic unit, into a highly centralized and unified industrial order in which the corporation is the economic unit.... To suppose that a decentralized political order operating under a traditional separation of powers and checks and balances can effectively control a centralized economic order, or even act as a counter-check, is to ignore the facts of economic and political life.

Insofar as social welfare concerns stem from economic conditions, they are likely to transcend state boundaries. Interventions contained by state lines are less likely to be effective than those initiated uniformly nationwide.

Further, Kennedy (1981:21EY) argues that the federal government, which alone is the political organ of all the population, has undertaken many praiseworthy initiatives, has been the nation's conscience in pursuing collective ideals above regional and state parochialisms, and has developed centralized administration as a highly evolved mechanism. "To dismantle it haphazardly," he concludes, "in the name of a possibly antiquated 'localism' is more than modern America should be made to endure."

A second critical concern surrounding decentralization under the new federalism is the extent to which decisions actually will be made closer to communities and include the people affected by them. Lehman (1978:17) maintains that

> a bureaucracy is a bureaucracy regardless of geographical proximity....
> There is no guarantee that a local bureaucracy is more responsive, sensitive,
> or effective than a remote one. Moreover, [decentralization] inevitably

elaborates bureaucratic layers rather than diminishes them. . . . The fact that, in American history at least, local power has been more corrupt, less professionally competent, and more particularistic seems to complicate matters further.

In addition, much of the literature on citizen participation in welfare decision-making at state and local levels indicates that the level of participation is generally low and that typical participants are mobile, articulate, and only marginally needy (e.g., Kotler, 1969; Street et al., 1979; Miller et al., 1980). If bringing decisions closer to beneficiaries is a linchpin in the rhetoric of new federalism, it is not a particularly strong one.

Even if a large number of constituents could be mobilized to take part in social welfare decision making, broad participation has its drawbacks. Some writers note that participation by diverse citizens or interest groups leads to policy dilution in order to achieve some form of concensus (Rein and Rabinovitz, 1978; Lowi, 1974). As a consequence, tough decisions are not likely to be made, and priorities are not likely to be set. One negative latent outcome of participation is apt to be enhanced competition between narrow interest groups vying over limited funding resources for narrow demands (Lowi, 1969). Another possible negative outcome is legislation as ambiguous as that promulgated at the federal level.

In sum, the new federalism gets mixed reviews. While certain states may be in better structural position to assume welfare responsibilities than they have been in the past, they are not at a fiscal advantage. Further, it is questionable whether states should shoulder welfare problems that have been caused by nationwide forces. Finally, the prospect of decision making closer to home is an unconvincing argument for the new federalist approach to the sharing of welfare responsibilities.

What does all of this mean for direct service provision? How do these larger structural, fiscal, and philosophical issues impact the everyday lives of service personnel and, by extension, their clients? Returning to the categories of complaint presented in Chapter 2, it can be seen that at least three types of difficulties are exacerbated by the new federalism. The most obvious problem is the lack of resources, both in terms of service funding and provider time. Insofar as states are unable or unwilling to make up for the loss of federal funds for human services, difficulties associated with inadequate funds will increase. Certain providers are more likely to experience this crunch than others: those working in cities of states where suburban interests dominate the legislature, individuals residing in financially poorer states, and those who serve the minority groups of a state. An increased feeling of lack of time may be experienced by service workers asked to mobilize clients for public hearings and other local advocacy activities, especially if such activities fail to show any appreciable results.

The new federalism promises, at least in its transitional phase, to heighten the ambiguity of service workers' jobs. After the first year of experimentation with block grants, state and local administrators had not worked out a smooth division of labor with federal authorities regarding the responsibilities of the various levels of government. In some cases state officials have been uncertain about what decisions they can make and have declined a leadership role in welfare activities. Certain states have experienced disputes between the legislative and executive branches of state government over who will allocate block grant monies. Local governments that have been accustomed to dealing directly with Washington about various issues have had to develop relations with the state (Peterson, 1982). Whatever ambiguities exist at the state level are bound to be passed down to direct service providers in the form of continually changing mandates, rules, and regulations.

Further, just because Washington removes itself from the funding of certain services does not mean that service workers' paperwork responsibilities will diminish significantly. Accountability to the federal government will continue in those areas in which it retains jurisdiction. While the Reagan administration had promised regulatory relief, early analysis of moves in that direction suggest only limited relief for public agencies. The removal of various rules and regulations has occurred more readily for the private sector than for public initiatives. For example, Washington has not shown a reluctance to promulgate even further guidelines for AFDC (Eads and Fix, 1982). It is largely in the area of block grants that regulations and reporting requirements at the federal level will be substantially reduced (Peterson, 1972; Gutowski and Koshel,

1982). In addition, because state legislators are closer to the people to whom they are responsible, they may end up requiring accountability procedures as elaborate as those that providers have experienced from the federal government.

Finally, decentralization may contribute little to clarifying the boundaries and procedures of service work. Federal legislators do not monopolize the prerogative to create ambitious, ambiguous, or fragmented legislation. Chapter 4 discussed the difficulties these policy characteristics generate for service workers. An additional factor at the state level contributes to the confusion providers have about their work. In states that have not undergone the structural changes noted earlier, allocation decisions may be made on the basis of favoritism and tradition rather than on the basis of demonstrated program performance. Because of such funding criteria, agency administrators may ask providers to give priority to agency activities that curry political favor. Such priorities, however, may conflict with what providers believe to be of primary importance, thereby heightening their work ambiguities.

In short, responses to the fiscal crisis at the federal level and attempts to shift certain welfare activities to the states will have significant impact on the ability of direct service workers to carry out their jobs. The four areas of complaint that are already frustrating to service personnel, difficulties with clients, problems with the employing agency, lack of resources, and mandates, rules, and regulations, will be rendered even more troublesome.

Service workers are presently experiencing a crisis of their own. How they will respond to it is problematic. On the one hand, it is possible that they will continue to employ personalized stress management techniques in order to get through the work day. Part of their coping may include a gradual lowering of their own expectations about public commitment to social welfare:

> The longer public-expenditure difficulties continue, the easier it should be to dissipate political frustration, since the general public will learn from experience to expect smaller and smaller increases in public expenditure. The heightened public discussion of budget "cuts" [that is, a reduction in expected increases] itself creates an expectation that spending should be reduced—and ordinary people are likely to interpret this to mean an actual reduction in constant- [or even current-] value money. A second

alternative is that continued economic difficulties will lead to the expectation of no increase in public spending in constant-money terms: a "nil
norm" can thus replace an expectation of continued public spending
growth. (Rose, 1980:227)

In effect, the present assault on welfare expenditures could provide the emotional innoculation (Janis and Mann, 1976) necessary
for relegating future retrenchment or line-holding measures to
the status of routine events. Should this prove true for service
providers, they will have conceded their altruistic concern for
optimal service performance to adaptive responses to lowered
welfare commitments.

On the other hand, the presence of a crisis state in social
services could provide the impetus for important reevaluations of
the current welfare system. As Schick (1980:124) suggests, "policy
officials might take advantage of the crisis for a new burst of
planning in which the purposes and capabilities of the government were reexamined and its priorities recast." If it is indeed a
time of reordering, it might be important to consider various
options to improve circumstances for service providers, as well as
their clients. In the final section some ideas and measures that
might offer ways out of the service trap are surveyed.

STRATEGIES FOR CHANGE

In Chapters 3 and 4, it has been argued that sources of workers'
dissatisfactions are located at least in part in the organization of
service work and in the policies that guide its everyday execution.
Therefore, those locations must be examined for possible sources
of change, as well. First the more limited strategies for change in
the form of policy alternatives will be examined. This is followed
by a discussion of changes in the nature of service work itself.

Changes from Above

If significant worker dissatisfactions derive from the nature of
the welfare policies they implement, then certain policy alternatives should be considered. However, exploration of these alternatives must be undertaken with some degree of caution. First, that

the measure of a good social welfare policy is a contented service worker is not being argued. Providers represent only one of several constituent groups, including clients, program administrators, bureaucrats throughout the implementation apparatus, and politicians, whom policies affect. The impact of policies on service workers as a group may or may not be a central concern of policy evaluation.

Second, policies affect these groups differently. For example, what may seem a favorable policy characteristic for service workers can nevertheless create dysfunctions for service recipients or for politicians. Accordingly, Cherniss (1978) reports that the use of special intake procedures with clients to prevent staff from being overwhelmed only added to the layers of bureaucracy facing a potential service recipient. On the other hand, certain measures intended to improve the situation for clients may do so at the expense of service workers. For example, research on means of improving service delivery to clients receiving home care demonstrated that improvements in the delivery system involved an increase in the time caseworkers spent per client in order to coordinate new and dispersed service components (Jette et al., 1981).

Third, single policies can contain inherently conflicting messages based on equally valued principles. In the most abstract terms, these take the form of rhetorical appeals for incompatible goals such as freedom and equality. At the concrete level, conflicts appear in forms such as service regulations that call for priority attention to the neediest in a population at the same time that service providers are expected to generate a certain percentage of program costs from client donations. In either case, while there may be the desire to espouse both or several principles simultaneously, joint implementation of such principles may often be logically or practically impossible.

Consequently, decisions regarding policy alternatives should be made with the realization that constituent trade-offs are involved. Decision makers may not find it in their interest to alter policies for the purpose of improving the situation of service workers; such policy changes may generate dysfunctions for other groups about whom the decision maker has concern. Indeed, policy alternatives may not even be endorsed by the workers whose situations they are meant to improve due to certain latent functions changes might produce, including deleterious consequences for the client.

With these considerations in mind, policy alternatives that would address specific problems experienced by service providers will be looked at. The policy characteristics generating difficulties for service workers include ambitiousness and symbolism, universalism, ambiguity, and fragmentation. Given fiscal retrenchment and the push toward decentralization, the time is apt to challenge all of these orientations. Instead of settling for across-the-board cuts in social programs, it is appropriate to ask anew "Who should be assisted, and in what manner?" Addressing this question directly demands priority setting for limited resources and nullifies the opportunity for decision makers to hide behind overly ambitious and ambiguous legislation. It also transforms the current hand-wringing responses about retrenchment into a creative opportunity to realign a welfare system that has grown large not so much by grand design as by political expediency.

Making hard decisions about target groups and allocations will generate at least short-term political discomfort. However, failure to address the impact of the fiscal crisis on the welfare system in a comprehensive way will have negative consequences, as well. Some likely outcomes from piecemeal welfare retrenchment include the alienation of diverse interest groups and the continuation of hundreds of underfunded welfare efforts that are structured for failure.

Concrete alternatives have been offered both from within the staffs of Congress and from outside the official realms of welfare decision making. These proposals range from a guaranteed minimum income in lieu of the myriad of assistance and service programs now in place to a graduated system of in-kind supports based on need (e.g., *Future Directions*, 1980). Common themes that run through these and similar proposals for overhaul of the welfare system are (a) the need for more specific targeting of service beneficiaries based on explicit criteria of eligibility, (b) definitive priority setting regarding types of services available instead of enabling legislation for a host of service possibilities, and (c) greater reliance on enhancing the care-taking and assistance capacities of personal support systems, such as the family.

The latter theme coincides with the call for moving away from a services strategy (e.g., Estes, 1979) wherein the government provides in-kind benefits, to a.system of financial support and tax incentives for families either to obtain a service from a range of market options or to supply it themselves in return for certain forms of tax relief. In effect, government-provided services would be residual in nature, but perform vital and specific gap-filling functions. Income supports must be at a level that assures recipients access to the marketplace. Otherwise, service recipients prefer in-kind benefits to cash assistance (Stuart, 1975).

An appropriate public welfare strategy may consist of a mix of activities: guarantee of a flow of cash assistance adequate for dignified subsistence, regulation of prices or cost containment in selected sectors to enable recipients of cash benefits access to the marketplace, provision of tax incentives for service provision by informal support networks, and maintenance of residual discretionary government services at the state or local level only where necessary. This kind of mix would address several problems. First, a specified level of income for all persons could be assured through an easily and directly implemented strategy comparable to a tax return. This would replace elaborate filters of means-testing to access an array of assistance programs. Second, reliance on informal support networks would remove the expectation from social workers to fulfill the socioemotional as well as instrumental needs of many clients. Third, what services remain would be tailored to the particularistic needs of a community due to the fact of discretionary decision making at the state or local level. Given limited resources, these services should focus on life-sustaining over life-enhancing assistance (Nelson, 1980) both as a matter of practicality and because of the need to set limits to the scope of government interventions. As Lowi (1979) urges, decision makers should become accountable for welfare decisions by prohibiting them from foisting policy without law upon bureaucrats and service providers. To achieve this the merits of a welfare mix such as outlined here might be debated.

To be sure, the various constituents of welfare policies stand to lose from some of the changes proposed here: politicians will have to concede the political credits and mileage they have heretofore extracted from interest groups through attention to their presumably specialized plights; bureaucrats, agency administrators, and direct service providers stand to lose their positions if a welfare reorganization de-emphasizing a services strategy were put in place; service beneficiaries and their families could no longer expect the government to supply particular services. On the other hand, the general mix of strategies suggested here may be a reasonable approach to addressing the needs and problems of these same constituents: politicians would be better able to evaluate welfare effectiveness because of definitive goals and objectives; service providers' and administrators' work would be less ambiguous and their clientele more delimited; clients would no longer be confronted with a massive welfare puzzle when trying to locate needed assistance, and those who are able to find assistance through their own personal relationships would no longer be penalized. In important respects, then, serious reform could alleviate many welfare difficulties without placing disproportionate hardships on any of the beneficiaries of the welfare system. Reform is timely, as well: the broad outline of change put forth here need not be more expensive, and may be more cost-effective, than the current maze of token efforts.

Changes from Within

Social welfare policies may change, but their alteration alone will not free workers from the service trap. The hierarchical structure of service work itself contributes to the difficulties experienced by line staff. Service providers carry out policies that are not of their making, are frequently inadequate, and often contribute to the dependency of clients on them and the service system. For a variety of reasons including their precarious status, service workers have been reluctant to "insist on the impossibility of their tasks" (Rainwater, 1967:64), have failed to "educate the communities to accept their limits" (Larson, et al., 1978:564), and have been disinclined to express the "righteous indignation" their circumstances provoke (Whitney Young, quoted in Trattner, 1979). However, the current atmosphere of debate regarding human services affords the opportunity for them to do so with perhaps less likelihood of reprisal than in times past. Further, it gives them the chance to reevaluate their own orientations toward the work they do.

As Bryan (1980:22) notes, "[I]n trying to make a better world, we often fail to start with the one thing we can really do something about: our own lives." There are a variety of changes workers could institute with regard to their positions and their routines within a service agency that collectively could transform the welfare system in significant ways.

Transformation will have begun when service workers acknowledge that their daily frustrations are based on public issues, not personal troubles. That is, the problems they encounter are not isolated events based on individual shortcomings but are difficulties experienced across service activities that stem from basic structural and political contradictions in society at large. This realization, rather than allowing workers simply to shift blame for adverse circumstances, can enable them to obtain a broader perspective on their work and generate broader proposals for change.

The cognitive shift to understanding daily complaints as public issues is most likely to come about as workers talk to one another about their situations. This can be facilitated informally in serious group discussions with colleagues and formally through membership in service worker caucuses and unions. Certain drawbacks to these collective activities should be noted. In the former case, the point will be missed if workers use discussion groups simply to blow off steam or unload complaints for personal catharsis. In the latter case collective potential will not be realized if objectives fail to go beyond self-interests such as reductions in caseloads or higher salaries. To be sure, these are reasonable objectives, but the larger public is more likely to be mobilized by qualitative issues such as improved service delivery, not quantitative ones (O'Connor, 1973). Further, the fruits of achievement will be short-lived if the broader context of the service structure goes unchallenged (*see* O'Connor, 1973; Galper, 1975; and Olson, 1982).

In addition, workers could help one another understand the political nature of their frustrations and support one another in instituting small changes in the workplace. The changes ultimately might add up to a reorganization of service work itself. For example, workers could press for the institutionalization of meetings among all levels of agency personnel for the legitimized airing and discussion of difficulties, grievances, and means of resolving them. Collectively workers could seek greater determination of agency policy commensurate with the important vantage point their line staff positions afford. (*See* Galper [1975] and Galper [1980] for a fuller discussion of these and related points.) Further, workers could press for the recognition and sanctioning of political advocacy as an expected part of their work responsibilities. Immediately workers should oppose federal regulations restricting lobbying by nonprofit groups (Ridgeway, 1983).

Insistence on such measures by an individual staff member might be interpreted by an administrator as the demands of a lone disgruntled employee and might even lead to informal negative sanctions against that worker. It is far more difficult, however, to ignore or seek reprisal against a solid core of like-minded workers, even in times of personnel retrenchment. Indeed, given the crisis state of many human service agencies today, workers could offer these suggestions in the spirit of innovative responses to difficult times rather than presenting themselves as adversaries to equally beleaguered agency administrators.

Transformation of the service system will also have been initiated when workers become oriented to an egalitarian relationship with their clients. The ability to perceive one's clients as one's equals has three important consequences. First, it will lead to service workers' insistence that clients become as self-sufficient as possible. This will reduce workers' complaints about overly dependent recipients.

Second, such a perception will make it easier for service workers to see that their plight and that of their clients are politically interconnected and that their respective difficulties stem from a common source. That source is a political economy that renders both providers and clients as surplus population. In effect, both are recipients of the benefits, however meager, of the welfare state. Both are dependent upon a public and its decision makers who are ambivalent toward the roles that they play; further, the public and politicians are content to assuage their guilt about the needy by foisting concern over the day-to-day exigencies of need on the shoulders of a well-motivated, but underfunded and ill-guided, cadre of service personnel. Any shortcomings of the welfare system are then easily blamed on either of the parties in the provider-client relationship rather than on the parties originally responsible for welfare inadequacies.

Third, the ability of workers to view clients as equals makes both mutually valuable allies in whatever political struggles are undertaken (Lipsky, 1980; Galper, 1975; O'Connor, 1973). While social workers have a legacy of political activity, it is not clear that they are politically influential (Mathews, 1982). Gaining allies for political activism might alter the degree to which politicians take service providers seriously. For such political cooperation to be meaningful in transforming the welfare system and the service trap, it must not waste whatever moral leverage it develops (e.g., Lowi, 1979). Any joint political action must be based on a broad analysis of the nature and sources of welfare problems, not on providers' manipulation of clients to serve their or their agency's limited political or organizational ends. Political cooperation in the past has taken forms such as providers' refusal to implement repressive welfare policies that wrest dignity and privacy from clients (Galper, 1975), or, more recently, workers' participation in voter registration drives to enfranchise the unemployed and the poor (Pear, 1983). This alliance could also be enlisted to press for the complementary array of welfare assistance described in the preceding section. If Piven and Cloward (1982) are correct in their analysis, the assault on social welfare by the Reagan administration might be just the impetus workers and clients need to form a mutually beneficial political alliance.

In conclusion, there are ways for workers to emerge from the service trap and, in so doing, to leave a legacy of welfare policy and ideals commensurate with the high expectations they held upon entering their work. To accomplish this, they will have to harness and sustain the energies dedicated to helping others to help themselves and their colleagues at the same time. As human service workers come under attack from political conservatives and liberals alike and from a discontented public seeking ready scapegoats, not to mention from some of the very clients they serve, it becomes all the more imperative for them to view their situations and their dissatisfactions in the context of broader societal dynamics. Through such a transformation of thought it is possible to use day-to-day dissatisfactions as windows to the larger world of political relations and cultural dynamics. This being the case, the "human drive for a more decent world" (Galper, 1975:77) can start anew from an improved vantage point and with a larger vision of what is possible through the social welfare enterprise.

Appendices

Appendix A

RESEARCH DESIGN

The core data base for this study consists of twenty-three intensive semistructured interviews with service providers in the field of aging. The respondents are social service personnel whose responsibilities bring them into direct contact with service recipients, in this case, the aging. Funds for the operation of programs and services provided by the interviewees derive largely from the federal government through the Older Americans Act. The settings in which the respondents work are either fully public or nominally private, nonprofit community agencies. All agencies for which the respondents work are located in a metropolitan area, as are the clientele who receive agency services. The specific types of positions held by respondents in this study include caseworker, nutritionist, information and referral specialist, transportation worker, meals on wheels coordinator, employment coordinator, senior center director, programming specialist, and nursing home ombudsman.

Respondents varied with regard to age, sex, race, education and training, size of agency for which they work, length of time in their current position, and reason for entry into service work. Demographic variations are detailed in Table I. Detailed and prolonged analysis of the qualitative data did not suggest that these variables significantly influence workers' perceptions of or dissatisfactions with their work or their general strategies for dealing with the problems of their work. Rather, what is significant for the arguments presented in the preceding chapters is the commonality across these variables of work-related problems and coping patterns.

The fact that all of the interviewees for this study work in organizations whose clientele are primarily older people deserves some attention in light of the argument throughout the preceding

141

Table I
DEMOGRAPHIC CHARACTERISTICS OF INTERVIEW RESPONDENTS (N = 23)

Age	
< 30	6
30–39	7
40–49	4
50–59	2
60+	3
Not reported	1
Sex	
Female	17
Male	6
Race	
White	15
Black	8
Education	
High school	4
Some College	4
College graduate	13
Not reported	2
Length of Time in Present Position	
< 1 year	5
1–2 years	6
3–5 years	6
Over 5 years	4
Not reported	2

chapters that the issues presented are pertinent to social welfare workers in general. While the direct quotations utilized throughout derive from a select group of social service personnel, their generalizability is demonstrated by referencing literature in other service areas. In addition, it has been shown that public welfare work in general is characterized by discernible patterns of social relationships and bureaucratic imperatives; further, public welfare policy is influenced by broad public opinion and common political needs. The assumption underlying this book is that the worlds of personnel in the field of aging, whose interviews provide the primary data base for the book, are, in important ways, similar to their counterparts in other publicly funded agencies addressing other categories of clientele.

Interviews with the twenty-three human service workers were conducted from September 1980, to February 1981. The timing of the interviews was a critical concern. It was essential to conduct all interviews within a period during which there were no significant policy or organizational changes that might affect the respondents' immediate perceptions of their work. During these five months a succession of the presidency from Jimmy Carter to Ronald Reagan was witnessed, an event with major implications for social welfare activities. However, this event was not able to make its impact in that time frame on the everyday world of service work; indeed, most social service changes as a result of new federal orientations would not begin appearing until October 1981, with the implementation of the first budget of the Reagan administration. Similarly, no extraordinary intraagency changes occurred during the time of the interviews.

Each interview was conducted in private by a graduate student trained in semi-structured interviewing procedures. The interviews ranged in length from forty-five minutes to approximately three hours and covered issues focusing largely on work satisfactions, work-related problems, and means of problem resolution. (The interview guide is found in Appendix B.) The utilization of this methodology with service practitioners enabled several important lessons to be learned:

First, by the very nature of their work, direct service providers have little discretionary time for interviews. It is advisable not to try to conduct the interview between client appointments or during the actual occurrence of a programming activity; this approach virtually guarantees a rushed interview characterized by minimal time for probing by the interviewer and the necessity of attenuated responses by the interviewee. Rather, it is best to schedule the interview during the provider's lunchtime, after work, or while the individual ordinarily would be engaged by inside-the-agency tasks, such as paperwork or other administrative duties.

Second, as an ongoing activity of the research project, the researcher should monitor the quality of responses coming from various questions or jumping-off points of the interview guide. As with any interview schedule or questionnaire, those items failing to yield rich data should be removed from future interviews.

While this is a common practice of most research, it bears repeating here because of the pervasive sense of lack of time experienced by the service workers interviewed. Thus, one may have to sacrifice repeated rephrasings of questions that typically provide checks on the respondent's consistency or understanding of the question.

Third, obtaining interviews may require unanticipated persistence on the part of the interviewer. This research problem derives from the nature of direct service work that, to an important degree, is unpredictable from one day to the next. The first request for an interview may be made on a bad day and result in refusal. A second call at a later date, however, may find the worker feeling either less rushed or more willing to talk about the job. Of course, two refusals should signal the researcher to find a substitute interviewee. Experience suggests that an initial reluctance or refusal may be a matter of reaction to one's immediate circumstances rather than an ongoing òrientation toward participating in a research project.

Fourth, ongoing refusal to participate may be based on fear of lack of confidentiality or anonymity in the research, particularly by potential respondents who find their work situations highly troublesome or who fear for their job. Insofar as this occurs, the final group of interviews obtained may in fact represent a conservative view of service work difficulties.

Finally, the researcher should be aware of the predictable timetables of service work that may interfere with his/her ability to obtain permission for interviews. Each agency operates according to several of the following types of schedules and deadlines: local budgets, state budgets, public hearings, routine evaluations, monthly recordkeeping and reports, and special holiday-related events. Knowing when these time-bound activities occur and avoiding such times in seeking interviews will save considerable energy in the research enterprise.

INTERVIEW GUIDE

1. Describe the work you do. (Probe if necessary for type agency, position, functions.)
2. How long have you done this kind of work? How long have you been in the particular job you now have with this organization/agency?
3. Why did you decide to do this kind of work?
4. What are the satisfactions and rewards you receive from this work? In other words, what do you like about it?
5. What are the problems with or the drawbacks about this work? In other words, what do you dislike about it?
6. What were your expectations about this job before you took it? Have there been any surprises or disappointments? How have you coped with these?
7. If there were some things you could change about your work, what would they be? How would you change them?
8. Do you feel that you have enough opportunity in your work to use the skills that you have? (If not, why not?) Is your work challenging?
9. Do you feel that you have enough opportunity in your work to make decisions? (If not, why not?)
10. How important is your work to you, in comparison to all of the other things you do? Has it always had this degree of (un)importance?
11. Please describe the clients (participants/recipients/consumers, etc.) you work with to me.
12. In your work, do you ever have demands made on you that cause stress or conflict? (Please describe them to me). How often do you experience these? How do you resolve those situations? How do you usually feel about the way those situations are resolved?

13. How do you feel that your job rates in the minds of most people in the community? (Why do you think they feel that way?)

14. Do you ever feel frustrated by your work? How do you cope with such situations? Do any of your coworkers ever experience frustration? (Please describe.)

15. Are you ever dissatisfied with how much you are able to accomplish with and for your clients? How do you handle that dissatisfaction?

16. Are there any characteristics of the policies under which you work that make it difficult to do your job well?

17. Do you ever feel exhausted by your work? How do you cope with such situations?

18. Are there ever occasions that you have negative feelings toward the clients you serve? (Please describe.) Are there ever occasions that you have highly positive feelings toward the clients you serve? (Please describe.)

19. What does the term "occupational burnout" mean to you? Have you ever experienced it yourself? (When?) How did you handle it? Do you think any of your coworkers have ever experienced burnout related to their work? Are supervisors sensitive to the possibility of burnout? (Please describe.)

20. Given what you know now about this job, if you had it to do all over again, would you take a job like this? (Why or why not?)

Interviewer's Note: The terms "work" and "job" are used interchangeably here. We would like responses, however, that address both the nature of the work as a function, and the characteristics of the particular structure of the job.

REFERENCES

Alfaro, Jose, and Holmes, Monica: Caveats and cautions: Title XX group eligibility for the elderly. *The Gerontologist,* 21:374–381, 1981.

Alutto, Joseph A., Hrebiniak, Lawrence G., and Alonso, Ramon C.: Variation in hospital employment and influence perceptions among nursing personnel. *Journal of Health and Social Behavior,* 12:30–34, 1971.

Arendt, Hannah: *Eichmann in Jerusalem: A Report on the Banality of Evil.* New York, Viking, 1964.

Armour, Philip K., Estes, Carroll L., and Noble, Maureen L.: The continuing design and implementation problems of a national policy on aging: Title III of the Older Americans Act. In Hudson, Robert B. (Ed.): *The Aging in Politics: Process and Policy.* Springfield, Thomas, 1981.

Arnoff, Franklyn N.: Social consequences of policy toward mental illness. *Science,* 188:1277–1281, 1975.

Avant, W. R., and Dressel, P. L.: Perceiving needs by staff and elderly clients: the impact of training and client contact. *The Gerontologist,* 20:71–77, 1980.

Ayers, B. Drummond, Jr.: The "new federalism" looks good—from Washington. *New York Times* (December 6, 1981):E–3.

Bailey, Stephen K., and Mosher, Edith K.: *ESEA: The Office of Education Administers a Law.* Syracuse, Syracuse University, 1968.

Baker, Frank: From community mental health to human service ideology. *American Journal of Public Health,* 64:576–581, 1974.

Balanced budget law poses threat to nation. *Senior Citizens News* (July, 1982):1–2.

Bardach, Eugene: Reason, responsibility, and the new social regulation. In Burnham, Walter Dean, and Weinberg, Martha Wagner (Eds.): *American Politics and Public Policy.* Cambridge, MIT, 1978.

Beam, David R., and Colella, Cynthia C.: The federal role in the eighties: bigger, broader, and deeper or smaller, trimmer, and cheaper? In Levine, Charles H., and Rubin, Irene (Eds.): *Fiscal Stress and Public Policy.* Beverly Hills, Sage, 1980.

Bechill, W. D., and Wolgamot, I.: *Nutrition for the Elderly: The Program Highlights of Research and Development Nutrition Projects Funded Under Title VII of the Older Americans Act of 1965, June, 1968, and June, 1971.* AOA, DHEW Publ. No. SRS 73-20236, Washington, D.C., 1972.

Becker, H. S.: Social class variations in the teacher-pupil relationship. *Journal of Educational Sociology,* 25:451–465, 1952.

147

Bergmann, Barbara R.: Charity needs coercion. *New York Times* (December 13, 1981):3F.

Billingsley, Andrew: Bureaucratic and professional orientation patterns in social casework. *Social Service Review, 38*:400–407, 1964.

Billingsley, Andrew, Streshinsky, Naomi, and Gurgin, Vohnie: *Social Work Practice in Child Protective Services.* Berkeley, University of California School of Social Welfare, 1966.

Binstock, Robert H.: Federal policy toward the aging—its inadequacies and its politics. *National Journal, 10*:1837–1845, 1978.

Binstock, Robert H., and Levin, Martin A.: The political dilemmas of intervention policies. In Binstock, Robert H., and Shanas, Ethel (Eds.): *Handbook of Aging and the Social Sciences.* New York, Van Nostrand Reinhold, 1976.

Bittner, Egon: The police on skid-row: a study of peace-keeping. *American Sociological Review, 32*:699–715, 1967.

Black, Chris: Welfare workers told: stop trying to match people to jobs. *The Boston Globe,* (August 24, 1982):21–22.

Brager, George, and Holloway, Stephen: *Changing Human Service Organizations.* New York, Free Press, 1978.

Brewer, Colin, and Lait, June: *Can Social Work Survive?* London, Temple Smith, 1980.

Broadway, Bill: Business unhappy over Reagan's call to increase charity. *The Atlanta Journal/The Atlanta Constitution* (February 28, 1982):1D, 6D.

Bryan, William L.: Preventing burnout in the public interest community. *The Grantsmanship Center News,* 9:15ff., 1981.

Bucher, R., and Schatzman, L.: The logic of the state mental hospital. *Social Problems, 9*:337–349, 1962.

Career burnout—or, inhumanity in the human services. *Behavior Today,* (October 6, 1980):4–7.

Chalfant, J. P., and Kurtz, R. A.: Factors affecting social workers' judgments of alcoholics. *Journal of Health and Social Behavior, 13*:331–336, 1972.

Cherniss, Cary: Recent research and theory on job stress and burnout in helping
· professions. Unpubl. ms., 1978.

Cherniss, Cary: *Professional Burnout in Human Service Organizations.* New York, Praeger, 1980a.

Cherniss, Cary: *Staff Burnout: Job Stress in the Human Services.* Beverly Hills, Sage, 1980b.

Cherniss, Cary, Egnatios, Edward S., Wacker, Sally, and O'Dowd, William: The professional mystique and burnout in public sector professionals. In press.

Cherniss, Cary, and Krantz, David L.: The ideological community as an antidote to burnout in the human services. Unpubl. manuscript, n.d.

Clymer, Adam: Governors to bargain on program swaps. *New York Times* (February 24, 1982):14A.

Collins, Randall: On the microfoundations of macrosociology. *American Journal of Sociology, 86*:984–1014, 1981.

Cook, Fay Lomax: *Who Should Be Helped? Public Support for Social Services*. Beverly Hills, Sage, 1979.

Cumming, Elaine: A sociological afterword. In Dunham, H. Warren (Ed.): *Social Realities and Community Psychiatry*. New York: Human Sciences, 1976.

Dahl, Robert A.: Decision-making in a democracy. *Journal of Public Law, 6*:279–295, 1958.

Dehlinger, J., and Perlman, B.: Job satisfaction in mental health agencies. *Administration in Mental Health, 5*:120–139, 1978.

Drucker, Peter F.: Managing the public service institution. *The Public Interest, 33*:43–60, 1973.

Dunham, H. Warren: *Social Realities and Community Psychiatry*. New York, Human Sciences, 1976.

Eads, George C., and Fix, Michael: Regulatory policy. In Palmer, John L., and Sawhill, Isabel V.: *The Reagan Experiment*. Washington, D.C., Urban Institute, 1982.

Edelman, Murray: *Political Language: Words That Succeed and Policies That Fail*. New York, Academic, 1977.

Edelwich, Jerry, with Brodsky, Archie: *Burn-out: Stages of Disillusionment in the Helping Profession*. New York, Human Sciences, 1980.

Edington, Bonnie Morel: The paradoxes of health planning. *Journal of Sociology and Social Welfare, 7*:359–373, 1980.

Emener, William G.: Professional burnout: rehabilitation's hidden handicap. *Journal of Rehabilitation, 45*:55–58, 1979.

Ephross, Paul H., and Reisch, Michael: The ideology of some social work texts. *Social Service Review, 56*:273–291, 1982.

Estes, Carroll L.: *The Aging Enterprise*. San Francisco, Jossey-Bass, 1979.

Estes, Carroll L.: Constructions of reality. *Journal of Social Issues, 36*:117–132, 1980.

Estes, C. L., and Gerard, L.: Salient political issues and emerging trends in the 1978 reauthorization of the Older Americans Act. Unpubl. ms., n.d.

Estes, Carroll L., and Noble, Maureen: Paperwork and the Older Americans Act: problems of implementing accountability. Staff Information Paper, U.S. Senate Special Committee on Aging. Washington, D.C., U.S. Government Printing Office, 1978.

Etzioni, Amitai (Ed.): *The Semi-Professions and Their Organization*. New York, Free Press, 1969.

Etzioni, Amitai: Old people and public policy. *Social Policy, 7*:21–29, 1976.

Federal spending up; state spending down. *Atlanta Journal and Constitution* (February 13, 1983):9A.

Finch, Wilbur A., Jr.: Social workers versus bureaucracy. *Social Work, 21*:370–375, 1976.

Fiske, Edward B.: Survey of teachers reveals morale problems. *New York Times* (September 19, 1982):1,40.

Fosler, R. Scott: Local government productivity: political and administrative potential. In Levine, Charles H., and Rubin, Irene (Eds.): *Fiscal Stress and Public Policy*. Beverly Hills, Sage, 1980.

Fraley, Phyllis: Volunteers may soften funds cuts. *The Atlanta Journal/The Atlanta Constitution* (November 28, 1982):1C,19C.

French, John R. P., and Caplan, Robert D.: Organizational stress and individual strain. In Marrow, Alfred J. (Ed.): *The Failure of Success.* New York, AMACOM, 1972.

Freudenberger, Herbert J.: Staff burn-out. *Journal of Social Issues, 30*:159–165, 1974.

Freudenberger, Herbert J.: The professional and the human services worker: some solutions to the problems they face in working together. *Journal of Drug Issues, 6*:273–282, 1976.

Freudenberger, Herbert J., and Robbins, Arthur: The hazards of being a psychoanalyst. *The Psychoanalytic Review, 66*:275–295, 1979.

Friedman, Norman L.: Cookies and contests: notes on ordinary occupational deviance and its neutralization. *Sociological Symposium, 11*:1–9, 1974.

Fritz, Dan: The Administration on Aging as advocate: progress, problems, and perspectives. *The Gerontologist, 19*:141–150, 1979.

Future Directions for Aging Policy: A Human Service Model. U.S. House of Representatives, Select Committee on Aging, Subcommittee of Human Services. Comm. Pub. 96-226. Washington, D.C., U.S. Government Printing Office, 1980.

Galper, Jeffry: *Social Work Practice: A Radical Perspective.* Englewood Cliffs, Prentice-Hall, 1980.

Galper, Jeffry H.: *The Politics of Social Services.* Englewood Cliffs, Prentice-Hall, 1975.

Glasser, William: *Positive Addiction.* New York, Harper and Row, 1976.

Goode, William J.: A theory of role strain. *American Sociological Review, 25*:483–496, 1960.

Gouldner, Alvin W.: The secrets of organizations. In The National Conference on Social Welfare: *The Social Welfare Forum, 1963.* New York, Columbia University, 1963.

Greenhouse, Linda: The fall and rise of the 10th amendment. *New York Times* (January 17, 1982):E–9.

Gross, Edward: Work, organization and stress. In Levine, Sol, and Scotch, Norman A. (Eds.): *Social Stress.* Chicago, Aldine, 1970.

Groves, James E.: Taking care of the hateful patient. *New England Journal of Medicine, 298*:883–887, 1978.

Gubrium, Jaber F.: *Living and Dying at Murray Manor.* New York, St. Martin's, 1975.

Gustafson, James M.: Professions as "callings". *Social Service Review, 56*:501–515, 1982.

Gutowski, Michael F., and Koshel, Jeffey J.: Social services. In Palmer, John L., and Sawhill, Isabel V. (Eds.): *The Reagan Experiment.* Washington, D.C., Urban Institute, 1982.

Halmos, Paul: *The Faith of the Counsellors.* New York, Schocken, 1970.

Handler, Joel F., and Hollingsworth, Ellen Jane: *The "Deserving Poor": A Study of Welfare Administration.* Chicago, Markham, 1971.

Hargrove, E. C.: *The Missing Link: The Study of the Implementation of Social Policy*. Washington, D.C., Urban Institute, 1975.

Harris, Robert J.: States' rights and vested interests. *Journal of Politics, 15*:457–471, 1953.

Helmer, D'Arcy J.: Iatrogenic intraorganizational processes as one mediator of burnout. In Morgan, Robert F. (Ed.): *The Iatrogenics Handbook: A Critical Look at Research and Practice in the Helping Professions*. Toronto, IPI, 1982.

Herbers, John: States want a deal with Reagan, but not this deal. *New York Times* (February 21, 1982a):4E.

Herbers, John: Congress survey finds cities using property tax to absorb losses in aid. *New York Times* (October 17, 1982b):12.

Herbers, John: Legislators and governors battle for control of U.S. block grants. *New York Times* (January 17, 1982c):1,17–A

Herbers, John: Shift to block grants raising issue of states' competence. *New York Times* (September 27, 1981):1,20.

Hewitt, John P., and Hall, Peter M.: Social problems, problematic situations, and quasi-theories. *American Sociological Review, 38*:367–374, 1973.

Holden, Constance: Nader on mental health centers: a movement that got bogged down. *Science, 177*:413–415, 1972.

Howe, Elizabeth: Legislative outcomes in human services. *Social Service Review, 52*:173–188, 1978.

Howe, Elizabeth: Public professions and the private model of professionalism. *Social Work, 25*:179–191, 1980.

Hudson, Robert B.: Rational planning and organizational imperatives: prospects for area planning in aging. *Annals of the American Academy of Political and Social Science, 415*:41–54, 1974.

Hudson, Robert B., and Binstock, Robert H.: Political systems and aging. In Binstock, Robert H., and Shanas, Ethel (Eds.): *Handbook of Aging and the Social Sciences*. New York, Van Nostrand Reinhold, 1976.

Huttman, Elizabeth D.: *Introduction to Social Policy*. New York, McGraw-Hill, 1981.

Janis, Irving L., and Mann, Leon: Coping with decisional conflict. *American Scientist, 64*:657–667, 1976.

Jette, Alan M., Branch, Laurence G., Wentzel, Richard A., Carney, William F., Dennis, Deborah L., and Heist, Marcia Madden: Home care service diversification: a pilot investigation. *The Gerontologist, 21*:572–579, 1981.

Kadushin, Alfred: *Child Welfare Services*. New York, Macmillan, 1974.

Kanter, Rosabeth Moss: *Men and Women of the Corporation*. New York, Basic, 1977.

Karger, Howard J.: Burnout as alienation. *Social Service Review, 55*:270–283, 1981.

Kennedy, David M.: U.S. centralism, yes. *New York Times* (October 25, 1981):21EY.

Kerson, Toba Schwaber: The social work relationship: a form of gift exchange. *Social Work, 23*:326–327, 1978.

Klemmack, David L., and Roff, Lucinda Lee: Public support for age as an eligibility criterion for programs for older persons. *The Gerontologist, 20*:148–153, 1980.

Kotler, Milton: *Neighborhood Government: The Local Foundations of Political Life.* New York, Bobbs Merrill, 1969.

LaRossa, Ralph, and LaRossa, Maureen Mulligan: *Transition to Parenthood: How Infants Change Families.* Beverly Hills, Sage, 1981.

Larson, Charles C., Gilbertson, David L., and Powell, Judith A.: Therapist burnout: perspectives on a critical issue. *Social Casework, 59:*563–565, 1978.

Latimore, James: Social services in the iron cage. *Journal of Sociology and Social Welfare, 6:*756–769, 1979.

Lehman, E. W.: Sociological theory and social policy. In Etzioni, Amitai (Ed.): *Policy Research.* Leiden, Brill, 1978.

Levy, Gerald: "Acute" workers in a welfare bureaucracy. In Offenbacher, Deborah I., and Poster, Constance H. (Eds.): *Social Problems and Social Policy.* New York, Appleton-Century-Crofts, 1970.

Lewis, Harold: The battered helper. *Child Welfare, 59:*195–201, 1980.

Lewis, J. David, and Weigert, Andrew J.: The structures and meanings of social time. *Social Forces, 60:*432–462, 1981.

Lipsky, Michael: Standing the study of public policy implementation on its head. In Burnham, W. Dean, and Weinberg, Martha Wagner (Eds.): *American Politics and Public Policy.* Cambridge, MIT, 1978.

Lipsky, Michael: *Street Level Bureaucracy.* New York, Russell Sage, 1980.

Lofland, John: *Analyzing Social Settings.* Belmont, Wadsworth, 1971.

Lowi, Theodore J.: *The End of Liberalism: The Second Republic of the United States,* 2nd ed. New York, Norton, 1979.

Lowi, Theodore, J: Interest groups and the consent to govern: getting the people out, for what? *Annals of the American Academy of Political and Social Science, 413:*86–100, 1974.

Lubove, Roy: *The Professional Altruist.* New York, Atheneum, 1969.

Lyman, Stanford M., and Scott, Marvin B.: *A Sociology of the Absurd.* New York, Appleton, 1970.

McKinlay, John B.: Clients and organizations. In McKinlay, John B. (Ed.): *People-Processing: Cases in Organizational Behavior.* New York, Holt, Reinhart, and Winston, 1975.

Marks, Stephen: Culture, human energy, and self actualization: a sociological offering to humanistic psychology. *Journal of Humanistic Psychology, 19:*27–42, 1979.

Marks, Stephen R.: Multiple roles and role strain: some notes on human energy, time, and commitment. *American Sociological Review, 42:*921–936, 1977.

Maslach, Christina: Burned-out. *Human Behavior, 5:*16–22, 1976.

Maslach, Christina: The client role in staff burnout. *Journal of Social Issues, 34:*111–124, 1978.

Maslach, Christina: The burn-out syndrome and patient care. In Garfield, C. (Ed.): *Stress and Survival: The Emotional Realities of Life-Threatening Illness.* St. Louis, Mosby, 1979.

Maslach, C., and Jackson, S. E.: Lawyer burn-out. *Barrister, 8:*52–54, 1978.

Maslach, Christina, and Jackson, Susan E.: Burned-out cops and their families. *Psychology Today, 12*:58–62, 1979.

Maslach, Christina, and Pines, Ayala: The burn-out syndrome in the day care setting. *Child Care Quarterly, 6*:100–113, 1977.

Mathews, Gary: Social workers and political influence. *Social Service Review, 56*:616–628, 1982.

Matthews, Sarah H.: Participation of the elderly in a transportation system. *The Gerontologist, 22*:26–31, 1982.

Mennerick, Lewis A.: Client typologies: a method of coping with conflict in the service worker-client relationship. *Sociology of Work and Occupations, 1*:396–418, 1974.

Merton, Robert K.: The role set: problems in sociological theory. *British Journal of Sociology, 8*:106–120, 1957.

Miller, A., Gurin, P., and Gurin, G.: Age consciousness and political mobilization of older Americans. *The Gerontologist, 20*:691–700, 1980.

Mills, C. Wright: *The Sociological Imagination.* New York, Oxford University, 1959.

Morris, Robert: Government and voluntary agency relationships. *Social Service Review, 56*:333–345, 1982.

Morris, Robert: *Social Policy of the American Welfare State.* New York, Harper & Row, 1979.

Muller, Thomas L.: Regional impacts. In Palmer, John L., and Sawhill, Isabel V. (Eds.): *The Reagan Experiment.* Washington, D.C., Urban Institute, 1982.

Munson, Carlton E., and Balgopal, Pallassana: The worker/client relationship: relevant role theory. *Journal of Sociology and Social Welfare, 5*:404–417, 1978.

Nelson, Gary: Social services to the urban and rural aged: the experience of area agencies on aging. *The Gerontologist, 20*:200–207, 1980.

Nelson, Gary: Contrasting services to the aged. *Social Service Review, 54*:376–389, 1980.

Netting, F. Ellen: Secular and religious funding of church-related agencies. *Social Service Review, 56*:586–604, 1982.

Nordhaus, William: Creeping "economic constitutionalism". *New York Times* (December 27, 1981):3F.

O'Connor, James: *The Fiscal Crisis of the State.* New York, St. Martin's, 1973.

Ogren, Evelyn H.: Public opinions about public welfare. *Social Work, 18*:101–107, 1973.

Olson, Laura Katz: *The Political Economy of Aging.* New York, Columbia University, 1982.

Oriol, William E.: "Modern" old age and public policy. *The Gerontologist, 21*:35–45, 1981.

Pear, Robert: New voter drive aims at unemployed and welfare recipients. *New York Times* (January 2, 1983):9.

Pear, Robert: Governors begin talks on federalism proposal. *New York Times* (March 7, 1982):28.

Peters, B. Guy: Fiscal strains on the welfare state: causes and consequences. In Levine, Charles H., and Rubin, Irene (Eds.): *Fiscal Stress and Public Policy*. Beverly Hills, Sage, 1980.

Peterson, George: The state and local sector. In Palmer, John L., and Sawhill, Isabel V. (Eds.): *The Reagan Experiment*. Washington, D.C., Urban Institute, 1982.

Peyrot, Mark: Caseload management: choosing suitable clients in a community health clinic agency. *Social Problems, 30*:157–167, 1982.

Pines, Ayala, and Kafry, Ditza: Occupational tedium in the social services. *Social Work, 23*:499–507, 1978.

Pines, Ayala, and Maslach, Christina: Characteristics of staff burnout in mental health settings. *Hospital and Community Psychiatry, 29*:233–237, 1978.

Pins, Arnulf: *Who Chooses Social Work? When and Why?* New York, New York Council on Social Work Education, 1963.

Piven, Frances Fox, and Cloward, Richard A.: *Regulating the Poor: The Functions of Public Welfare*. New York, Vintage, 1971.

Piven, Frances Fox, and Cloward, Richard A.: *The New Class War*. New York, Pantheon, 1982.

Pressman, Jeffrey L., and Wildavsky, Aaron: *Implementation*, 2nd ed. Berkeley, University of California, 1979.

Rainwater, Lee: The revolt of the dirty-workers. *Trans-Action, 5*:2ff., 1967.

Registt, W.: *The Occupational Culture of Policemen and Social Workers*. Washington, D.C., American Psychological Association, 1970.

Rein, Martin, and Rabinovitz, Francine F.: Implementation: a theoretical perspective. In Burnham, Walter Dean, and Weinberg, Martha Wagner (Eds.): *American Politics and Public Policy*. Cambridge, MIT, 1978.

Rein, Mildred: Fact and function in human service organizations. *Sociology and Social Research, 65*:78–93, 1980.

Ridgeway, James: Conservatives go after non-profit social service agencies. *The Atlanta Journal and Constitution* (July 31, 1983):11–C.

Ritzer, George: *Man and His Work: Conflict and Change*. New York, Appleton-Century-Crofts, 1972.

Robin, Stanley S., and Wagenfeld, Morton O.: The community mental health worker: organizational and personal sources of role discrepancy. *Journal of Health and Social Behavior, 18*:16–27, 1977.

Rochefort, David A.: Progressive and social control perspectives on social welfare. *Social Service Review, 55*:568–592, 1981.

Rogers, David L., and Molnar, Joseph: Organizational antecedents of role conflict and ambiguity in top-level administrators. *Administrative Science Quarterly, 21*:598–610, 1976.

Rose, Richard: Misperceiving public expenditure: feelings about "cuts." In Levine, Charles H., and Rubin, Irene (Eds.): *Fiscal Stress and Public Policy*. Beverly Hills, Sage, 1980.

Rooney, James F.: Organizational success through program failure. *Social Forces, 58*:904–924, 1980.

Roth, Julius A.: Some contingencies of the moral evaluation and control of clientele: the case of the hospital emergency service. *American Journal of Sociology, 77*:839–856, 1972.

Ryan, William: *Blaming the Victim.* New York, Pantheon, 1971.

Salamon, Lester M., and Abramson, Alan J.: The nonprofit sector. In Palmer, John L., and Sawhill, Isabel V. (Eds.): *The Reagan Experiment.* Washington, D.C., Urban Institute, 1982.

Sarata, B. P. V., and Reppucci, N. D.: The problem is outside: staff and client behavior as a function of external events. *Community Mental Health Journal, 11*:91–100, 1975.

Sarbin, Theodore R., and Allen, Vernon L.: Role theory. In Lindzey, Gardner, and Aronson, Elliot (Eds.): *The Handbook of Social Psychology,* 2nd ed. Reading, Addison-Wesley, 1968.

Schelling, Thomas C.: Command and control. In McKie, James W. (Ed.): *Social Responsibility and the Business Predicament.* Washington, D.C., Brookings, 1974.

Schick, Allen: Budgetary adaptations to resource scarcity. In Levine, Charles H., and Rubin, Irene (Eds.): *Fiscal Stress and Public Policy.* Beverly Hills, Sage, 1980.

Schwartz, M. S., and Will, G. T.: Intervention and change on a mental ward. In Bennis, W. G., Benne, K. D., and Chinn, R. (Eds.): *The Planning of Change.* New York, Holt, Rinehart, and Winston, 1961.

Scott, Marvin, and Lyman, Sanford: Accounts. *American Sociological Review, 33*:46–62, 1968.

Scott, Robert A.: The selection of clients by social welfare agencies: the case of the blind. *Social Problems, 14*:248–257, 1967a.

Scott, Robert A.: The factory as a social service organization: goal displacement in workshops for the blind. *Social Problems, 15*:160–175, 1967b.

Scott, W. Richard: Professional employees in a bureaucratic structure: social work. In Etzioni, Amitai (Ed.): *The Semi-Professions and Their Organization.* New York, Free Press, 1969.

Seabrook, Charles: Plight of Medicaid recipients bleaker. *The Atlanta Journal* (October 22, 1982):28.

Sieber, Sam: Toward a theory of role accumulation. *American Sociological Review, 39*:567–578, 1974.

Sieber, Sam: *Fatal Remedies: The Ironies of Social Intervention.* New York, Plenum, 1981.

Simpson, Richard L., and Simpson, Ida Harper: Women and bureaucracy in the semi-professions. In Etzioni, Amitai (Ed.): *The Semi-Professions and Their Organization.* New York, Free Press, 1969.

Smith, Kathleen Maurer, and Spinrad, William: The popular political mood. *Social Policy, 11*:37–45, 1981.

Specht, Harry: British social services under siege: an essay review. *Social Service Review, 55*:593–602, 1981.

State and local AAA's gear up for new contributions campaign. *Aging* (July–August, 1982):2–7.

Stebbins, Robert: Role distance, role distance behavior and jazz musicians. In Brisset, Dennis, and Edgley, Charles (Eds.): *Life as Theater: A Dramaturgical Sourcebook*. Chicago, Aldine, 1975.

Stokes, Randall, and Hewitt, John P.: Aligning actions. *American Sociological Review, 41*:838–849, 1976.

Storey, James R.: Income security. In Palmer, John L., and Sawhill, Isabel V. (Eds.): *The Reagan Experiment*. Washington, D.C., Urban Institute, 1982.

Stotland, E., and Kobler, A. L.: *Life and Death of a Mental Hospital*. Seattle, University of Washington, 1965.

Street, David, Martin, George T. Jr., and Gordon, Laura Kramer: *The Welfare Industry: Functionaries and Recipients in Public Aid*. Beverly Hills, Sage, 1979.

Stuart, Archibald: Recipient views of cash versus in-kind benefit programs. *Social Service Review, 49*:79–92, 1975.

Suttles, Gerald D.: Foreword. In Street, David, Martin, George T. Jr., and Gordon, Laura Kramer: *The Welfare Industry: Functionaries and Recipients in Public Aid*. Beverly Hills, Sage, 1979.

Thibaut, J. W., and Kelley, H. H.: *The Social Psychology of Groups*. New York, John Wiley & Sons, 1959.

Titmuss, Richard: *The Blood Relationship*. New York, Pantheon, 1971.

Toren, Nina: Semi-professionalism and social work: a theoretical perspective. In Etzioni, Amitai (Ed.): *The Semi-Professions and Their Organization*. New York, Free Press, 1969.

Trattner, William: *From Poor Law to Welfare State*, 2nd ed. New York, Free Press, 1979.

Wade, Richard C.: The suburban roots of the new federalism. *The New York Times Magazine* (August 1, 1982):20–21ff.

Warren, Roland L.: The interaction of community decision organizations: some basic concepts and needed research. *Social Service Review, 41*:261–270, 1967.

Wasserman, Harry: Early careers of professional social workers in a public child welfare agency. *Social Work, 15*:93–101, 1970.

Wasserman, Harry: The professional social worker in a bureaucracy. *Social Work, 16*:89–96, 1971.

Weisman, Steven R.: Reagan's new federalism — bold stroke or smokescreen? *New York Times* (January 31, 1982):1E.

Wells, Susan: Pilot workfare program put to test in 4 counties. *The Atlanta Journal* (November 8, 1982):1,2C.

Westley, W. A.: Violence and the police. *American Journal of Sociology, 59*:34–41, 1953.

Wilensky, Harold L., and Lebeaux, Charles N.: *Industrial Society and Social Welfare*. New York, Free Press, 1965.

Willie, C. V.: The social class of patients that public health nurses prefer to serve. *American Journal of Public Health, 50*:1126–1136, 1960.

Wilson, James Q.: The bureaucracy problem. *The Public Interest, 6*:3–9, 1967.

Wilson, R. N.: Patient-practitioner relationships. In Freeman, Howard E., Levine,

Sol, and Reeder, Leo G. (Eds.): *Handbook of Medical Sociology*. Englewood-Cliffs, Prentice-Hall, 1963.

Wolfensberger, Wolf: *Normalization*. Toronto, National Institute on Mental Retardation, 1972.

Wolman, Harold: Local government strategies to cope with fiscal pressure. In Levine, Charles H., and Rubin, Irene (Eds.): *Fiscal Stress and Public Policy*. Beverly Hills, Sage, 1980.

Zajonc, R. B.: Cognitive theories in social psychology. In Lindzey, Gardner, and Aronson, Eliot (Eds.): *The Handbook of Social Psychology*. Reading, Addison-Wesley, 1968, Vol. I.

Zerubavel, Eviatar: Timetables and scheduling: on the social organization of time. *Sociological Inquiry, 46*:87–94, 1976.

Zerubavel, Eviatar: Private time and public time: the temporal structure of social accessibility and professional commitments. *Social Forces, 58*:38–58, 1979a.

Zerubavel, Eviatar: *Patterns of Time in Hospital Life: A Sociological Perspective*. Chicago, University of Chicago, 1979b.

Zimmerman, D. H.: Tasks and troubles: the practical bases of work activities in a public assistance organization. In Hansen, D. A. (Ed.): *Explorations in Sociology and Counseling*. Boston, Houghton Mifflin, 1969.

NAME INDEX

SUBJECT INDEX

163